Charity
Means Love

Transforming the Culture
of How We Give

Nathan Monk

Charity Means Love
Transforming the Culture of How We Give

Nathan Monk

NathanMonkTour@gmail.com
CharityInstitute.com

ISBN-10: 0578425785
ISBN-13: 978-0578425788

Cover Photography: Copyright © 2018 Steven Gray
MoveMediaLLC.com

Cover design: Copyright © 2018 by Tashina Monk
TashinaJoy.com

Printed in the United States of America
First Edition

10 9 8 7 6 5 4 3 2 1

Dedication

Every word written here is dedicated to the passionate people who give their life in service to others. No matter where you fit in the grand scope of charity, from activism and volunteerism to board members and paid staff, you all give more than anyone ever sees and I hope that this work does justice to our collective hopes and dreams.

To my amazing and supportive family, both my parents and siblings, who helped refine my opinions in the furnace of love.

This would not have been possible without my amazing children, Kira, Selena, and Gideon, who inspire me every single day to try harder and to be better. And of course, their amazing mother, Tashina, who has taken me on as an act of charity in spite of my many shortcomings and the forever evolution of what it means to be co-parents.

Note

This book is a letter of love to all of those who serve in the wonderful network of charity throughout the world. Even though I use some examples in this book of areas that need improvement, this is not a condemnation of individual organizations. Many of the programs I mention in this book are already on a pathway towards improvement and others have already long abandoned practices they now see as unhelpful to their overall cause.

My hope and intent in telling these stories is to call us all to self-reflection and action. None of us have done it perfectly from the onset. We have all learned from our positive experiences and failures. So I hope that this work is not used as a battering ram to harm others. Rather, may we each use it as a guidepost for doing more and doing it better.

When we use love, compassion, and reason as our motivators, we can effect real and lasting change. Much of what we do in the world of nonprofit work is emotions based. We are responding to a crisis, whether it is housing loss, a medical emergency, or an unforeseeable act of nature. Because we work in crisis, which is always emotional, it is easy to take criticism of how we do things as an indictment against the heart in which we do them. Nothing I say here is an indictment of the heart, just a gentle call to all of us, myself included and foremost, to walk in mercy, lead with forgiveness, and hope for the future.

Foreword

Nathan Monk is the only white guy I know who smokes menthol cigarettes. I found that out the one time I got to meet him in person sitting at a table outside a bar in Pensacola. In the hour that the two of us spoke, maybe twenty or so people greeted Nathan from the sidewalk. Some of them were twenty-something bar rats; some seemed like they were probably homeless; some were blue collar workers heading home from their jobs. He sat there silently living the gospel of love through puffs of smoke. The thing I thought at the time was this guy Nathan Monk is a man of the people; he should run for mayor. I'm pretty sure if Jesus Christ lived in Pensacola, Florida today, he would sit outside smoking menthols and dapping with homeless people.

Nathan was isolated from the Eastern Orthodox priesthood because he went public with his support for gay rights. He's gotten in all kinds of trouble with institutions of every kind because of the renegade way that he goes about life, doing things like protesting panhandling ordinances and contradicting powerful businessmen in city council meetings. Nathan hasn't succeeded at everything he's done. But he's failed his way forward, to use the terminology of my friend the Christian mystic writer

Elaine Heath. He learns from his mistakes and grows wiser. I don't think I've known a more fearless risk-taker than Nathan. Because he knows what it's like to live on nothing, he's not terrified of having his world come crashing down like so many middle-class people are. And whenever the crashes come, he always comes out of the rubble stronger and more determined than ever before.

This book is full of rich stories and real, practical wisdom from someone who has given his life to living out the actual vocation of charity. Nathan has a lot to criticize about the Non-Profit Industrial Complex that has squandered its role in taking care of the neediest among us, but the most prominent tone in his writing is his compassion for the people he wants to see healed. As a Christian pastor of college students, I want for my students to understand what it means to take up your cross and follow Jesus. Nathan is on the shortlist of people who come to mind when I consider what examples of radical Christian discipleship I can put before my people.

His writing is wild, beautiful, and brutally authentic. If you're ever in Pensacola, ask some random homeless guy about Nathan Monk. I'm sure he'll have a great story. Or you can just read this book.

Rev. Morgan Guyton
Author, *How Jesus Saves the World from Us*

Preface

There is a coming economic crisis. I do not say this for shock value or out of some attempt of prophetic brilliance. This is not a statement of my own devices but rather facing the reality that some of the greatest minds in business have already warned, though few have listened. We are approaching a potential end to the steady economic growth that has emerged out of the crash we experienced a decade ago. Everyone from Jim Clifton to Tony Robbins and Gary Vaynerchuk have given mathematical and historic insight into the certainty of an end to the bull market we've been experiencing that has led to a roaring economic boom, a steady rise in employment, and a resurgence of entrepreneurship, the like of which we've not seen since our grandparents rose up out of the Great Depression. We do not know when the next crash will come, but signs of a volatile market are already beginning to present themselves. So whether that crash comes before this book reaches print or even a few years from now, the reality is that it is imminent.

What do business, entrepreneurship, and market volatility have to do with the non-profit industry? Absolutely everything. The basis of most charities that we experience today is built upon models created during the Great Depression, from soup kitchens to homeless shelters, medical resource centers, and so much more. More importantly, most of the laws regulating all of us who operate under the 501c3 heading are birthed out of a response to the Great Depression. The strength of those principles was tested when faced with the modern crisis of the crash of 2008—many organizations failed. Most non-profits had not evaluated themselves, their marketability or industry standards in decades. Once they were finally faced with a 21st century cry for help, they were forced to realize that they were ill equipped to respond using up-to-date processes. Many organizations were not even using modern computer-based programming or data collection, and they were light years behind in utilizing the internet to raise funds, responding to client needs or to express their mission to those who might want to volunteer. The majority of us have moved on to using apps on our smartphones to do, well, literally everything! Dating, buying clothing, concert tickets, and even our weekly grocery shopping is all done through apps on our phone. But the non-profit industry is just starting to learn how to build beta websites.

As other industries have experienced a rapid change in cultural response, a new wave of entrepreneurs have begun to step into the field of non-profit work, desiring to give back into the communities and causes that are important to them. However, these new givers are finding it hard to navigate a process that feels disconnected from the rest of the world. While nearly every business and business owner is engaging their clients and supporters through social media platforms like Snapchat, Instagram, and Facebook, non-profits rarely have an updated website and are far from engaged on these platforms. Many are still begging for traditional media to be their only boost to engage their message.

Most millennials are being cautious about where they shop, much less where they give. They want to know things like sustainability, community impact, the job place culture, and if the employees are being given adequate vacation time. And that's just what they want to know about the places they get their coffee from! As this new generation moves into becoming the businesses owners and soon-to-be donors, board members, and founders of local and national non-profits, they want to know more, engage more, and make sure that their dollar is making the biggest impact it can.

The world of business is preparing for the change. They are taking steps to evaluate their company culture, fundamentally changing the way that they communicate with their employees and clients. Some companies are giving unlimited mental health days, to make sure that folks are working at their own pace and taking the time they need to stay safe, healthy, and active, because a proactive approach to employee/employer relationships has proven time and again to bring forward people who are willing to do the best for their companies. In contrast, there are some non-profit executive directors who haven't taken an actual vacation in years. And the members of their board aren't the only ones responsible. There is a societal expectation that if you work in a given field, you should work yourself to the bone and never have time for leisure. We've got a cultural problem about how we address every aspect of giving.

The warnings have been put out there. Culture has to change, the way we engage with clients has to change, and, in spite of our best efforts, there will be another crash. So, if we listen to those in the business world, and prepare for whatever crisis, crash or calamity is coming, we can be ahead of the curve. Because when the inevitable comes, those of us who provide free or reduced services, including shelter, healthcare, legal aid or food, will become the most essential industry in the world—just like we were in 2008 and 1929. But if we do not prepare, if we don't listen and we don't learn, we will be part of the problem instead of the solution.

One of my mentors used to tell me, "You teach based on what you know." When I first began working with those experiencing homelessness, I did not realize how true of a statement that was. Back in the beginning, I looked at the world through a very narrow lens. I put the issues I was fighting for at the top of the pyramid of concern, I didn't spend much time thinking about environmental issues or cancer research. I would judge silently (and sometimes vocally) about how our society would pour so much money into these issues when we had people living on the streets. There seemed to be a disconnect. I would wonder, *How can there be anything more important than making sure people have access to food and are off the streets?* But there wasn't a disconnect; there was an intersection. Back then, I was operating a small food outreach program and fighting City Hall to keep them from shutting us down. I was running around in circles trying to keep something alive that, by all standards, was a Band-Aid on a bullet wound. And, yes, it was a very important Band-Aid. What I realized as I grew to have more experience is that it was really a Band-Aid on a never-ending nuclear war against the poor, the sick, and the marginalized. We were fighting against a scorched earth and there seemed to be no end in sight.

The stories I tell in this book are based upon what I know, because that is the only place from where I know how to teach. What I can see now, that I couldn't see back when I first began, is that the struggles for the non-profit industry are universal and, more often than not, intersectional. As I would begin to talk to folks coming through our food line, I would hear stories about individuals who had lost their job due to an oil spill or because their bodies were now failing because cancer was eating them away from the inside. Soon, I began to see that those of us on the front lines of fighting poverty and homelessness desperately needed these environmental activists and breast cancer researchers just as much as we needed fair housing initiatives. We were all working together to fight a universal enemy: injustice and inequality.

If all our agencies could work together and sing the same song of freedom, then many of those whom we were helping might have never have ended up on the streets to begin with. If my dear friend who works hard every single day to fight for regulations to protect the fishing industry were to succeed, then my other friend who was living on the streets would have never lost his job to begin with. My eyes were slowly opened to the reality that there was a connection, a missing piece, a profound synergy between what we were all attempting to accomplish.

The principles I speak about in this book are universal. Yes, I speak from my own experience and that experience is within the segment of the non-profit sector that addresses homelessness specifically, so these are the anecdotes I pull from. It is my story and the stories of those whom I've worked with on this particular battlefield along with the volunteers, case managers, executive directors, and clients. The ideas themselves are not limited to one demographic of the non-profit industry but are applicable to all of us who fill a need in our communities known as charity. Whether you are working with orphans or single mothers, if you are helping clients fight for mental health reform or you run a free clinic providing AIDS testing, there will be something here for you because I wrote this with each and every one of you in mind. You are my inspiration and muse. Your dedication, whether you are a board member, volunteer, receptionist, case manager or director, is profound and oftentimes underappreciated. You have all experienced these same stories in your particular field. Some of them have been heartbreaking and others have led to success. But what we all want, at the core of our work, is to streamline that success and create better systems that maximize our resources and make the lives of our clients better.

Every year I sit in small and dingy rooms as volunteers and staff from all areas of the community gather to begin the Point in Time (PIT) survey, the annual national count of those experiencing homelessness. It does not matter if I am in my own community or sitting in as a consultant in another town, the meetings always begin the same: "We know that there are problems with the PIT count. But it's the system we have." Does this sound familiar to your own work? All of us in the non-profit world have meetings just like this, things we are obligated to do or attend; things that don't light the fire under us and that somewhere, deep inside, we know may even be antithetical to the work we are attempting to accomplish. But we have to do them because grants require it, or we need the data for state funding, or some other reason outside of our control compels us to complete these tasks.

What I propose in this book is that there is a better way, one that releases us from compulsions and leads us on a journey toward liberation, both for ourselves and for those whom we are called to serve.

I use in this manuscript a Judeo-Christian theological context because, yet again, it is what I know. But these ideologies are also universal in their application. I am using terms that I grew up with, that I am familiar with, because that is my personal context. However, what I have learned over the years is that the idea of loving your neighbor, caring for the persecuted, and fighting for justice is not uniquely owned by the Christian faith. I have walked on picket lines with people of all faiths and also those who do not associate with any particular religious creed. When we all stand together, arms linked, holding back the power brokers from crushing those whom we are fighting for, our blood is all red, our tears are all made from the salt of the earth, and our cry is the same, regardless of our context.

This, for me, is a love letter for everyone I have fought alongside—the sojourners. It is for everyone who has helped open my eyes through patience and compassion, the ones who let me run directly into brick walls, even though they knew what was there, just so that I could learn my own lesson. This work is my part of the journey of striving for social reform so that non-profits can be more effective in their individual directives. It is not a complete pathway forward. Rather, it is a guide, a toolbox to pull from and design which portions best fit within your particular purpose and calling.

There are portions of this text that call out toxic activities within our system and some of them might be bitingly specific. I say them not out of hatred but as a way toward restoration. We cannot compel change through silence, nor can we bring light into darkness without fire. These stories I tell here, though I personify them, are because I've heard others list the same concerns. But those bringing these concerns forward are clients living on the streets or volunteers who truly care about the organization or even executive directors who feel powerless to speak out lest they lose their job. I speak out on their behalf, saying what they feel they cannot, so that hopefully we will all take a moment to listen because many of the mistakes I list in these pages I have been guilty of myself. So let us grow together and find a better way forward.

The thesis of this work is love. Each charity was born out of love. We become aware of a crisis and respond to the need. Charity is often born out of tragedy. We lose a loved one to cancer or AIDS. We watch as a dear friend is eaten alive by addiction. A child is abducted from a loving family and then they are faced with the worst news imaginable, their child has been lost forever. A momentum is built around tragedies. Volunteers march, search or scream. So what do we do with those beautiful people who now feel a void? We start a non-profit; we appeal to our legislatures; we fight. We fight because we love. Nearly every single non-profit was born out of this; someone experienced a loss, or saw someone struggling, and we responded with a big bleeding heart to the need right before our eyes. I hope that you will find imbedded in this work a way to keep that love alive and to no longer allow bureaucracy to weigh us down; that the law of love will transcend the rules we've allowed to plague our system and that prevent us from focusing on our original mission, whatever that individual mission might be for you.

My hope is simply this: may this call us all back to love, the place where we all began.

Contents

CHAPTER ONE

Charity Is

We Are Full of Ourselves

The blade was pressed firmly against my neck and my eyes were locked with my would-be killer's. I knew his name and his story because, just moments before he flicked his switchblade, he was my friend. His street name was Skunk, due to a Jay Leno style white streak of hair that cut directly down the middle of his pitch-black mane. I reacted quickly to disarm him and, with the help of a friend, we detained him as we waited for the police to arrive. The situation had escalated to this point because Skunk felt that I had betrayed him in some way. In his mind, I had violated the code of the street and I was about to pay the penalty given for betrayal within the justice system of the underbelly. Before this moment, I had been to him

1

a resource and also a friend. The reality was, in spite of the food and blankets and other menial help I had been able to provide, I had not been able to fix the underlying issues of his homelessness. This situation forced me to betray something else, my own personal ideology. Here I was, having to send someone to jail. I was stuck between my responsibilities to this individual I cared about and my responsibilities to everyone else who was in my care. *Why isn't there another option?* I wondered within my heart.

In the naivety of my youth and inexperience, I had believed that I was doing the best I could. And in many ways I was. I was doing the best available to me within a system that is intrinsically broken. We look at addressing homelessness as providing food, clothing or other temporary solutions, but hunger isn't homelessness, it's hunger, and needing clean clothing isn't homelessness either. Though these things are symptoms of the broader issue of poverty, they are not unique to homelessness. They are simply exterior problems that need to be addressed and, more importantly, are the triage, not the cure.

This extends into all aspects of how we respond within the framework of what my friend Mike calls the Non-Profit Industrial Complex. Those might sound like heavy words, but the truth is so much of how we respond within our system of charity is addressing the symptoms instead of the cure. How do we make a fundamental change in approach? We have got to stop looking at the output and instead focus on outcomes.

So many of us measure our success by how many people we've given blankets to or how many cans of beans we've given out in a month. I don't say this with a sense of judgment because it's how I operated as well. Then I began to look at folks who were doing things differently, they were breaking the mold and achieving an entirely unique level of success. For example, Mike runs a non-profit that provides an emergency campground to folks who are living in a state of homelessness and are being kicked off of private or government properties where their campsites were set up. However, when you ask him about his success, he rarely talks about how many people are currently living on the site or how much food they've provided daily. Instead, he begins to tell you about the people who have graduated out of his program and are now living in sustainable independent housing. It is not just a fundamental shift in mentality but in how we operate. We stop putting emphasis on the basic needs and patting ourselves on the back for meeting them. Instead, we focus on the end goal, which should always be the cure.

The thing is my knife-wielding friend should never have been on the streets to begin with. And if he wasn't on the streets, he would never have been put in the situation he was that night when he reacted out of his fear and desperation. There should have been a system in place where, from the first moment of him losing housing, he could have tapped into a supportive network and received help from day one. Instead, we have a complicated and convoluted set of programs that mainly focus on the exterior needs of survival and are not catching people before they fall. When someone is operating within survival mode, they are prone to pull knives on people that might cut them off from their means of survival. That's what fear does to us: causes us to respond in a primal way. Not because we are bad people but because that is quite literally what survival mode is. The whole basis of survival is, at its core, cutthroat.

Instead of Skunk being put in supportive housing or being provided a pathway back toward sustainability, he was carted off that night in a cop car. What I know now, that I didn't know then, is that if our society was shaped differently, for 1/3 of the cost our community would spend to keep him in jail just to face his trial for assault, we could have prevented him from ever being homeless in the first place. We could have cut this off at the pass and provided care when he first realized he was falling behind on bills, back when he lost his job, and long before he ever ended up on the streets.

Survival mode is not exclusionary to people living on the streets. We see it in every aspect of human suffering. We see it in clients who have to choose life-saving medication over food and then are forced to steal in order to eat. We see it in the mother who has to sleep in her car while her daughter is inside the hospital receiving medical care. The movie *John Q* was based off the story of a man, Henry Musaka, who attempted to take a hospital hostage in order to force them to provide care for his ailing son. These actions of desperation are, in their own way, acts of love. Misguided? Maybe. Whether they are love of self or love for another, when the ability to meet the needs of ourselves or those we care about becomes impossible, the human instinct of survival removes our ability to function within the logic of societal norms and instead makes us go to whatever extremes we deem necessary in order to find a way to continue on.

Charity is supposed to be the love that fills in the gaps. It holds the hand of the father who is afraid their child will not receive medical care and walks them through the process. It walks through the parking lots of the hospitals and finds the mother sleeping in her car and says, "We have a place for you." It catches you before you fall, before you spend a night on the streets, before your heart transplant, before you hear the diagnosis. It wipes away the tears and then finds a way to make sure they never have to fall again. That is what charity is supposed to be.

However, in our culture, the idea of charity has been inadvertently reduced to an action of how it makes the giver feel, and is not about the quantifiable results for the person on the receiving end of our alleged kindness. This statement is not made from a place of judgment about those who give but rather a need for us as givers to realize that this model is neither sustainable nor helpful for either party. When we give based upon how we feel, and not based upon actual need, disappointment sets itself in the heart of the giver. This happens because we've stopped looking at charity as an action of love for the person on the receiving end and more as a uniform protocol, a duty that we have to fulfill during the holiday season—forgetting, of course, that people are also in need of blankets, food, clothing, and hugs outside of the month between Thanksgiving and Christmas. Folks also live in destitution on May 23rd, but there is little emotional gratification or time to take a selfie on some random day of the week. We have regulated our giving around tax season or random emotional heart tugs, rather than being based on legitimate need or even whether or not our actions are producing life-changing results.

When I first began working in the non-profit sector, I started an outreach food distribution program. We met every Thursday evening in a local park and brought a hearty meal that was fried to Southern perfection. Because Thanksgiving always falls on a Thursday, I foolishly thought that this would mean that Thanksgiving Day would be our most highly attended event to date. We prepared over 200 meals. Our volunteers showed up with a little extra pep in their steps, that feeling of holiday cheer and gratitude for their own privileges showing in their smiles. Many of them had arrived from spending time with their friends and family, most of them commenting on how full they were but mentioning it in a compassionate context, acknowledging the juxtaposition that they were full but that they would soon be taking food to those who were unable to eat.

With careful motions, we diligently packed the perfectly manicured food, each plate individually boxed in Styrofoam to-go containers. Large pieces of fried chicken and homemade sides, we even packaged something new for today, a small piece of pie. I drove the main car down to the park where we met in the heart of downtown. Normally we had between 75 and 125 people waiting for us when we arrived. I could hear the Styrofoam containers squeaking against each other with every turn. It added to the soundtrack of anticipation we all felt as we got closer and closer to our moment of supplying our "homeless friends" with a very happy Thanksgiving dinner.

As I pulled up to the park, I was instantly struck with confusion. There was no one waiting in line. Normally by this time in the evening the park would be filled with bodies waiting for food. Park benches would be packed and the truly eager would have already formed a line in hopes that they would be able to quickly swoop back around and be lucky enough to get seconds. But the park was barren, not a soul in sight. My heart quickly sank into my stomach. For weeks we had been harassed by the local police and city officials. Had they chosen today, of all days, to finally scare everyone off? It almost seemed perfectly poetic.

Typical, I thought silently to myself.

Our caravan easily found parking places in this holiday created ghost town. We each slowly descended from our vehicles, looking at each other with confusion and worry. Then a moment of hope presented itself: A few of our friends came walking around the corner with their backpacks in tow. I took the initiative and ran up to them.

"You guys hungry?"

They looked at each other and laughed. "Monk, we ain't hungry."

"Well, we made a lot of food if you guys want something for later."

"I ate enough for a week, bro," another guy chimed in. "We started at the Episcopal Church then the Methodist."

"Then those ladies brought the hot dogs to the MLK park," his friend reminded him.

"Oh right, and we just ended at the mission. Bro, we're good. Real good."

They came and shook my hand and sort of leaned in for an awkward dude hug before they walked off with their packs and bikes and full bellies. I watched as they each waddled off in their turkey and hot dog induced bliss. The first guy lit a cigarette and turned back around to me.

"Yo, Monk!"

I quickly turned around with a smile, thinking maybe they would want seconds after all.

"We will be hungry tomorrow."

"And the day after that!" the second guy announced.

"Yeah man, everyone remembers us today. They'll remember us on Christmas. It's every other damn day we need the help. See you next Thursday."

"See you Thursday," I said with a defeated wave.

I began to learn an invaluable lesson that day, though it would take many years for the concept to fully penetrate my consciousness. I was thinking about myself rather than my friends that day. This was about invoking an emotional response for me, for our volunteers, and not about listening to the needs of the client. I should have asked if they wanted food on Thanksgiving. Furthermore, we should have coordinated with the other organizations working to distribute food that day. Instead, each organization worked as a lone ranger, seeking their own benefit. It wasn't about the client but about self-gratification for the volunteer and tapping into the heartstrings for potential donations to the respective non-profits. The people lost in the middle of all of this were the people we all claimed we were there to serve. They weren't listened to and instead walked away overstuffed and yet still worrying about food tomorrow. Our overabundance that day would not alleviate their long-term hunger, but it did quench our own personal thirst for self-importance.

That was the very last time we served food on Thanksgiving. It was time to listen to our friends and focus on the other 364 days of the year.

Want vs. Need

There was a tangible tension in the air as the council president read off action items in monotone form. Nearly everyone in the room was eagerly awaiting just one item to be called from the agenda. Each side of the room had organically segregated itself. On the left sat business owners in suits and ties and property owners in their Jimmy Buffet uniforms, all ready to lament how their quaint beach town was being taken over by bums. A young business owner who ran a jewelry store took to the microphone to talk about the fear that they and others felt having to pass by sleeping beggars on their way into work.

Across the way, to the right side of the aisle, sat a different cast of characters, almost equally stereotypical; young college-age activists, elderly college professors, and tattooed hipster pastors filled the microphone, speaking about love and hope and a future where folks could get help. The Bible was quoted a great deal by both sides, each finding a way to justify their opinions with the words of Christ. One man in opposition to the beggars said, "Jesus wouldn't want me to give to someone's addiction. I give to charities that will help the poor, actually help them! Not just a hand out—" he paused for emphasis "—but a hand up."

Both sides of this argument ultimately wanted the same thing, to see the beggars off the street. What they could not seem to agree on was the when, how and why. Those in opposition to panhandling wrongfully assumed that those requesting help on the streets were simply refusing help. Like most well-intentioned people, they assumed that there existed more than enough resources available for those experiencing homelessness and that those who were currently living, and more importantly begging, on the streets of our small coastal town must be doing so through simple stubbornness or because they were some kind of scammer.

"They choose this life!" many angry residents would scream that night.

I wished so deeply that I could have taken them to stand on those street corners and listen to the stories of those whom they condemned. Could they open their hearts and ears to the pleas of the poor? Is it possible to negate all of these stereotypes? Furthermore, how do we make them aware that, not only are these folks not trying to take advantage of the system, the system itself is broken. And, far worse, overcrowded and broken. No, there isn't enough room for all of these people, as one man claimed. In our small town there would be hundreds of folks that would look up at the stars that night and sleep in the muggy summer heat without shelter. They would go to sleep uncertain if they would be awakened by a police officer telling them to move on. Not because they were choosing this life over sleeping in a shelter but because the shelter was at capacity and, even if they could get a bed, they would only be allowed to stay there three nights a month. But how do I explain all of this reality to someone without sounding like I am condemning all of these charities?

Then a thought came to me. *Maybe it is time to call out the problems within our charity system, regardless of how it sounds.*

Not because I hate them or think that those who are choosing to volunteer their time or resources to these organizations are bad people! Rather because it seems that the Charity Industrial Complex has simply gotten too big for its britches and has little to show for it. We've reached a point where we've allowed output and not results to be the measuring stick of success. The goal of a homeless shelter shouldn't be how many mouths they've fed but how many people they've transitioned into permanent housing; not how many beds have been full but how many are soon going to be empty. We've gotten the whole idea backward and it's past time to face the music that maybe we've been doing this whole charity thing completely wrong.

It's alright to be wrong, just so long as we are willing to make it right.

Many years ago, I had a conversation with a businessman who was challenging my opinion on how to address panhandling in our community. To make his point, he used a personal anecdote about an experience he once had with a homeless man who he saw holding a sign. The individual was directly requesting money, but the businessman didn't want to give money. His excuse was typical; he didn't want his funds to be used on drugs or alcohol, which, of course wasn't true. This businessman actually loved to use his money on drugs and alcohol; he just meant he didn't want to pay for a homeless person's drugs or alcohol. Instead, he went across the street to a local pizza shop and purchased the man a pizza. He arrived and the panhandler seemed to be ungrateful for his gift. The businessman told me that, as he drove away, he saw the person throw the pizza in the trash. This was evidence enough for him that the panhandler was ungrateful, thus condemning all future folks he saw panhandling to be seen as equally ungrateful for his charity. Over the years I've heard similar stories from countless others and these memories are used as universal indictments against the poor.

The problem with this highly flawed perspective is that it's based upon the idea that we know better about the needs of the receiver than they do. We refuse to give money based upon the trope of the drug addicted beggar who only wants our money in order to get the next fix. And so this metaphorical figure looms over the actual needs of the real life people we meet. It becomes a justification for our lack of response to the genuine situations in front of us based solely on a figment of our collective societal imagination.

This stems from an idea that has saturated our cultural mindset, that if someone is in need, they cannot have wants, and that we as the giver can determine and distinguish between the two for another person without ever taking the time to listen to why they are asking in the first place. Everyone is judged against an idea of what society thinks homelessness is instead of looking at the unique circumstance of each individual experiencing it. We just assume that the request for money is based upon the reason our prejudice projects and that "our" money will be spent on something we wouldn't want it to be spent on, be it drugs, alcohol, candy or any other luxury of life. We forget, of course, that not everyone who drinks a beer is an alcoholic, not every homeless person is an alcoholic, and not every alcoholic is homeless. Even the poor are entitled to escapism from time to time, maybe even more so. As the scriptures say, "It is not for kings to drink wine, not for rulers to crave beer, lest they drink and forget what has been decreed, and deprive all the oppressed of their rights. Let beer be for those who are perishing, wine for those who are in anguish! Let them drink and forget their poverty and remember their misery no more."

I'm not suggesting that everyone should go around buying six packs and dropping them off at their nearest homeless camp, but what I am implying here is that we've created a mindset where only those who fit into the "haves" category are entitled to the pleasures of life and the "have nots" must perfectly play the part of squalor. If they do not, then we judge them and treat them with suspicion. This is two parts problematic because we are projecting future actions on someone we have not met and are also dictating the actual need based upon our own assumptions.

For this businessman, I shared a story in rebuttal and it's one that I have told many times.

Our community had been in the process of passing a number of anti-homeless ordinances and the topic had become very heated. These laws were the very source of the conversation I was having with this man. One of the most contentious points of the ordinance was the anti-panhandling section and the many constitutional and human rights problems it created. The very first person that I am aware of who was arrested under this new law was a woman named Stacey. She was old and heavy-set and very sick. She would call me often just to vent about her never-ending grocery list of medical ailments. I would sit there and listen to her explain in graphic detail about tooth infections and toes that would likely need to be amputated. She would end every call with, "One day, I hope, I'll call with good news." She never did.

One day, her call came from the county jail. She had been arrested for "flying a sign" and was in need of someone to bail her out. I worked throughout the night to find a way to post her bail. With the help of a local strip club owner and a very tired bail bondsman, I was able to help her escape her imprisonment in the late hours of the night (See: Rahab and Zacchaeus).

When Stacey was arrested, she was panhandling because she was in need of tampons and there didn't exist a single non-profit that supplied this essential need. Neither did the jail, we learned. So for hours she waited and bled and struggled with embarrassment and shame. Her crime was being a woman in need and her punishment was humiliation for being a human living in poverty. She was someone who didn't fit the need quota that we allow for the poor. How many people drove by her that day before the officer arrived and projected guilt upon her? They justified not giving in that moment because they told themselves, *Maybe she is on drugs,* even though they were wrong, she wasn't on drugs. Offering this woman a pizza would not have stopped her bleeding. She needed money, actual real money, to purchase a need that no one supplied. But society has taught us to view her another way, an incorrect way. We are told not to see her as a human with both wants and needs but simply as a beggar in need of the next fix.

She spent a night in jail, costing the tax payers thousands of dollars. Of course, the cost for Stacey was much steeper; the cleaning up of "blight" from our city sidewalks came at the cost of her humiliation. Sure, the street corner was momentarily cleared but at the price tag of her dignity, all because we have presumed incorrectly about Stacey and so many others.

It is past time that we change this mindset, not only because of how it effects our fellow humans who are in need but also because we are shooting ourselves in the foot by doing so. When we allow society to denigrate the homeless as all participating in criminal activities, this mindset is slowly used to justify making all other actions of survival that they do as criminal activities as well. Now that we have made human needs such as sleeping, having blankets or asking for assistance crimes, and when we punish these 'crimes' by putting people in jail, we have extended the circular aspects of poverty. And it all comes at a cost to everyone. The arrest, incarceration, public defender, and court costs come at a great expense. It has been estimated that an individual person experiencing homelessness can cost a community in excess of $60,000 dollars per person, per year, because of these and other expenses. I began to wonder, *Is it possible there might be a better and more effective use of those funds than someone spending thirty days in the county jail for falling asleep?*

The answer is undoubtedly yes and the results in those communities that have taken on the challenge have been beyond expectation.

Finding the Words

I am not a saint and I don't have any divine answers on tap. What I can offer instead is experience, accomplishments and, of course, failures. Just like you, at one point I didn't have the right words to define exactly what was wrong with how charity is supposed to function (or rather has stagnated in a state of dysfunction). But then, one day, because of a mistake on my part, the words found me.

There are few things as frustrating to a professional as forgetting the tools of your trade, only to realize you have done so once you've arrived on the scene of the job. For some professions this is more damaging than others. For me, on the day in question, I had forgotten my Bible and did not realize it until I had walked into a church that was not my own. I was scheduled to perform a wedding within five minutes of walking through the door. The verse I was to recite had sailed over my lips hundreds of times. However, there is something to be said about the theatrics of church, especially during weddings and funerals. These are the moments remembered throughout our life; people pay thousands of dollars to make sure that they are perfect. And one thing that they most assuredly expect is for the priest to stand there holding a Bible, not simply regurgitating words from memory.

I subtly made my way around this historic building trying to find a genuine Bible that was not hidden behind glass with some forefather's name etched on a faux gold plaque. Finally, I found a sufficiently beautiful leather-bound book. It was King James, which seemed rather archaic, but I didn't plan to actually read from it, just use it for glancing purposes just in case my mind betrayed me, which, I might add, happens far too often.

The wedding commenced, no one the wiser for my blundering mistake. "Rise, for a reading..." and I read the first verse with gravitas. But this wasn't the verse people were waiting for. They stood there with anticipation; it was almost 1 Corinthians 13 time. It was time for the love verse. Every halfway decent Christian can recount it nearly by heart. Rarely is it not the go-to for weddings just like this one, even some passive atheists like this verse at their weddings. It's so darn catchy. So, making my best priesty face, I looked down at my borrowed book and read aloud, "Charity suffereth long, and is kind."

Well, I had really messed that up! What kind of two-bit Bible was this anyways? I quickly rebounded and replaced charity with love and saved the day. I knew this verse front and back. I had this under control. But inside me an existential crisis was brewing.

Charity means love?

What does that mean for how we function as a society, and, most importantly, what does that mean for how we function as Christians? From the hyper-fundie to the Christmas-Easters, what do we do with the reality that charity is not simply something that we do but it's translatable to a feeling of the heart, with a biblical formula attached?

In my decades-long experience of working in an area people call charity I have seen the action of charity take two very hyperbolic forms. There are those who look at it with extreme passion, clambering after the idea of charity like Romeo for Juliet, a schoolboy romance without substance or meaning. It is here today and gone in the morrow. They are willing to even die for it in the moment, but as soon as the rush of hormones subsides they might think twice about the whole endeavor and they move on, chasing after the next pretty thing they see.

The second category, of course, is the extension that looks at charity very much like a business. It has finite rules and rituals. You must meet particular criteria in order to qualify for this thing or that. There is no room for emotions; it is the practical side of religion. Emotions are reserved for the ebb and flow of worship or other creative wings of the church. But charity is risky; some fear there might be abusers, users or, even worse, non-Americans, that might benefit from our charity without actually earning it.

I have seen both of these models within the traditional cultural context of love personified: marriage. I have seen those who chase after agape love with such force that they don't get to know the person with whom they are enamored. They are not looking at the whole person, they are not thinking of any relational reasons why they supposedly love the individual in front of them. This isn't about practicality, this is about emotion. Those marriages tend to fail in the same way this model of charity fails. They explode in a ball of flame and passion, leaving the embers to cool on the ground once the smoke finally settles.

The same is true of those who look at marriage or long-term relationships as merely a system of contracts, reconstructed debt, and getting children through college. Both of these types of relationships will produce results, just like enamored charity will see a certain number of people fed and purely pragmatic charity will see people fed as well. However, we need charity that acts a whole lot more like 1 Corinthians 13, a charity that is long suffering and kind, that is not envious or boastful or arrogant. We need charity that is not rude and doesn't insist on its own way, one that isn't irritable or resentful of those who need that charity, one that does not rejoice in wrongdoing but rejoices in truth and that bears all things, loves all things, hopes all things, and certainly endures all things.

We need charity that never ends.

So I invite you on this relationship counseling course for charity. It's time we went through one. Even strong relationships need to go through a bit of a tune-up from time to time. And, quite frankly, if any business operated the way that most charities do, they would have been closed down long before now. It's time to sit down, relax and air out some grievances. It's time for some tough love.

CHAPTER TWO

Patience

Never let your zeal outrun your charity. The former is but human, the latter is divine.
Hosea Ballou

Take a Breath

In a not-at-all uncommon moment, one of our volunteers canceled last minute at the shelter. I was the only full-time staff person and so whenever something didn't go as planned, it fell on my plate. On many a night I would end up having to fill in because a volunteer got a better offer, caught the flu or just forgot to show up. That is the nature of volunteerism. They are volunteering the time and so sometimes other parts of life get in the way. I rearranged some plans I had for that evening and packed up shop and went to stay up at the shelter to keep watch overnight.

We had recently moved in a mother and son that we didn't have room for. They were taking up residence in a space we called the living room. It was a common area with a television, games, and snacks. It was also the place where the overnight volunteers would hang out and occasionally nap. We did a lot of making room that year. This was the first time we had needed to use the living room and that meant I would be sleeping in the kitchen.

The building we had acquired was an old fellowship hall that had a large assembly room and then smaller rooms that were once used for Sunday school. We had nearly fifty people every single night, three bathrooms, and only one of them had a shower. We were maxed out. So were our volunteers. This evening it fell on me to fill in the gap. I grabbed a cot and blanket and rolled everything out neatly. The kitchen smelled of fifty years of fried chicken and loving grandmas preparing for church bake sales. I was exhausted.

That next morning, I cooked breakfast and waited patiently as the last guest finally left. I had hardly slept the evening before, tossing and turning as I could hear the chorus of snores echoing throughout the building. One of the residents down the hall was pregnant and she kept juice in the refrigerator in the kitchen; every thirty minutes or so she would knock on the door, asking for more juice.

When I arrived back at my house, I looked like death. I was disheveled and I had literal luggage under my eyes. Not bags, suitcases. I started to wonder where the line between insanity and executive director of a non-profit began and ended.

My phone rang.

I stared at that number for a long time. I hovered my thumb over the ignore button. It was one of my residents. I had just seen her not even a half hour before this as she jumped onto a bus to head to a job interview.

Couldn't this wait? I thought to myself, *Better yet! Why didn't she ask me this when she saw me this morning?*

"Hello?" I caved.

"Mr. Monk! I messed up bad. I came up here to the job interview and I left all my paperwork, résumé, I left my wallet with my ID. I don't know what to do!"

"Where are you?"

Within a few minutes, I was back in my car and driving back to the shelter and unlocking the door. Here I was all over again. I was beyond disoriented. However, I quickly found her documents placed neatly at the end of her bed. They even had a little note on them: "DON'T FORGET THESE." I drove them up to where she was scheduled to have her job interview, arriving just in time. She went inside with a smile on her face.

She got the job.

When we remove individuality out of our charity and outreach, we create a vacuum for disaster. Doing the hard work of looking at folks individually is more difficult and messy. It forces you to wake up in the middle of the night or go the extra mile. It takes patience and endurance. It's not easy. Beyond that, it forces you to break the rules or, better yet, never create unreasonable rules in the first place. But there sure are a lot of unreasonable rules that we place on folks that are trying to get help.

The problem is that most non-profits are built out of a singular vision of one person. Someone will get an idea and a board will be built around that initial plan. Rarely are non-profits built out of a think tank that takes the time to look at best practices and models for success, as you would with any other business or entrepreneurial endeavor. The problem with this is that these organizations tend to become cults of personality, and even more damaging, they tend to become stagnated with those damning words, "This is how we do it." Without the ability to learn, change, and grow, stagnation sets in and becomes septic. As society continues to evolve, so do the needs of those charities are meant to help. A perfect example of this would be a program that was invented by the White House in order to help people find jobs.

President Ronald Reagan authorized a program called Lifeline Assistance in 1984 and that program was designed to help individuals and families who were struggling financially. The idea was that, without a phone, how would someone be able to find a job? Lifeline was created so that those on government assistance could one day get off of that assistance by finding gainful employment. For decades this program remained stagnated, still offering landlines long after cell phones became the most popular way for people to communicate. It wouldn't be until the end of the second Bush Administration, and then carried out by the Obama Administration, that Lifeline was transitioned into the modern age and instead of supplying landlines they now provided a cheap cell phone with limited minutes on it. Just imagine how many more people would have had access to employment and other services had this program transitioned sooner!

Because charities oftentimes fall into this emotional and ideological rut, it is important that we take time to evaluate not only the danger that this presents to the organization as a whole but also to the clients that it is designed to serve.

There was a mission in my town that had become stuck in its own ways regarding a very important issue: Length of Stay. Almost any organization that provides transitional and emergency shelter has created length of stay caveats in their programming. Like most rules that are created by organizations, these rules come from a place of not wanting to allow people to abuse the system. The question then becomes, when does the "system" that we don't want people to abuse eventually become part of the problem itself (a perfect case of this being this mission)? They almost exclusively worked with the male population experiencing long-term, or chronic, homelessness and they decided to limit the amount of time a person could stay at the mission per month to only three nights. They also wouldn't take someone if they had been drinking or showed signs of drug use. This created a dangerous situation where the most vulnerable clients were left exposed. But it also opens up the broader question of what can someone really accomplish in three days of being housed, especially knowing that they will be thrown back out to the elements at the end of that time?

What we have slowly grown to understand is that the need to rush and cycle people though the system in order to make a bed available for the next client is not a manageable or effective model to follow. What do we accomplish for a client's longer-term health and stability by offering them a bed for a few nights or even a couple of weeks? Sure, we relieve the temporary suffering for a point in time, but that's truly all we've done. It is quite literally the definition of perpetuating the problem. And collectively we are spending millions of dollars a year locally and billions nationally in order to simply say we did something at all. However, the question becomes what value does a solution have if it doesn't accomplish a meaningful end result? All it has accomplished is creating a system that allows for the giver to feel as if they have done "their part" and move on, never asking what the end result might be.

Now, there is no doubt that there is a genuine emotional response for a volunteer when they come into a shelter or soup kitchen and slop food on someone's plate. That experience can even be eye opening for some individuals but at the expense of making the client essentially a zoo exhibit. A cautionary tale. We bring our children and grandchildren on holidays or during special events and stand behind glass food guards and throw food at the homeless.

It should be noted that no one is questioning that this system does provide food for people and that people getting food is positive and necessary. But we are gauging success in these scenarios completely wrong. We spend so much time worrying about keeping people alive that we stop worrying about quality of life. Yes, we need soup kitchens and rogue organizations that bring meals out to the streets. These are essential lifelines that must continue in order for basic survival needs to be met. However, communities as a whole have to stop allowing survival to be the status quo and start looking for proactive solutions that lead to the longer-term result of rehousing and sustainability. Sometimes these rehousing models will require forward thinking. You cannot, for example, reasonably expect a Vietnam veteran who has been homeless since he set foot back on American soil to simply move out of the woods and into traditional housing. It would be a shock to the system. This is why I believe the camp ground/group living/single dwelling, transition is the best and most cost-effective trifold system currently being used. It is a program based upon graduation and education, with a come as you are, housing-first core.

What is so important about having a delegated camping facility for those experiencing homeless is that it removes the first phase of the length of stay issue that we've seen fail. A campground acts as a first step toward moving out of homelessness for those who've been living outside for a long period of time. Many of those who have been living on the streets for a year or more have anxieties that prevent them from wanting to move back inside. In many communities around the nation, they are beginning to implement sanctioned campgrounds on the same campus as their traditional shelters. This model allows for there to be a space that a client can always be guaranteed to sleep at. It isn't perfect, it isn't fancy, but they have a safe space where they can always pitch a tent and lay their heads. This removes the fear of arrest for trespassing or even harassment by those who would want to terrorize a less fortunate person.

It should be noted that length of stay caveats are dangerous for all aspects of shelter and rehousing programming, whether it is a campground, boarding-house-style shelter or even transitional housing. Most people don't end up homeless based off of one singular action. So it is important to remember that if someone didn't end up homeless in one day, they are unlikely to get out of the situation in one day. Agencies that are seeing the most rehousing success are beginning to remove set time limits and instead opting to utilize case management to determine how long a person can or should stay. If someone is no longer afraid of their basic needs being met, food, shelter, a bathroom, then they are able to free up their mental space for other aspects of their recovery process: looking for a job, working on school, building credit or even substance abuse counseling when applicable.

All that happens when we try to use cookie cutters on humans is we end up with a lot of hurt and bleeding people. Not to mention that the old model is technically more expensive. When we don't treat the core issues causing someone's homelessness, be it mental illness, inadequate income or a background that needs to be cleaned up, then we just keep them circulating through the system. Year after year, the same people keep accessing the exact same services—food, emergency funding, blankets, shelters—and that comes at great expense. The sooner we get someone off of the street and back into the workforce or involved in whatever programs they are entitled to the sooner they are able to become a consumer. Each week, month, and year someone spends on the streets is another moment that they are forced to just cycle through a broken system. And who is that benefitting? Yes, taking on the challenge of actually helping address the individual issues of the total person often has a higher initial cost but produces long-term results that are measurable. We have to stop looking at charity within the context of the short term and emotions-based heart tugs and instead be patient and look toward the long-term goal: ending homelessness for our communities.

Think that sounds impossible? You would be wrong. This is true no matter the demographic your agency serves. We can innovate, we can create, we can empower. Even if the model of the system is broken, the needs of the community you serve are genuine. We can rework the system and make it client-based. You just have to be willing to pull out all the stops.

Stepping toward Success

In the summer of 2014, I was hired by a local entrepreneur to do a needs assessment for the City of Pensacola to determine what services were available and where the gaps existed. It became clear early on that there was a major need for families in the area of emergency shelter. After they looked at the entire analysis, they determined to launch a pilot program for shelter that would operate during the cold weather months. This gave us an opportunity to try out many of the models that we had observed working nationally. The motto that we used for the launch was simply, "No rules." It had become very clear that the exhaustive rules that had been created in most shelter programs acted as impediments to the clients' overall success. If we were going to implement rules at all, they would be new ones based upon the actual issues we would face in our own shelter and we would evaluate those based upon best practices that we saw exampled in other national programs that had achieved the type of success we hoped to see.

One of the first families we took in at the shelter was a single mother and her two young children who had moved to Pensacola from up north. She transplanted here because a family member had promised her a place to stay after they lost their family home to a fire. Immediately upon moving in with the family member, the landlord threatened eviction to the cousin if she didn't reduce the number of people living in the house. Not wanting both of them to end up homeless, she moved out without anywhere to go. She had been rejected by the only other family shelter in town because she didn't have identification.

This points directly to one of the major issues that many people experiencing homelessness run into. Most shelters and other programs require state issued identification. This can be a very difficult thing to come by when you are no longer able to meet the requirements to receive an ID, like having a permanent residence, birth certificates, and other things that you aren't likely to be carrying around in your backpack or the trunk of your car.

A good friend of mine used to work with veterans experiencing homelessness. He traveled directly into the camps to find out what they needed. He would bring them survival products and help them fill out their VA Benefits paperwork. One year, he met a guy who refused to fill out his paperwork, believing that he would be denied, but after months of convincing this veteran finally caved. To his amazement, a few months later, he had been approved for his benefits and was entitled to years of back pay from when he had originally filed. However, there was one major problem. He couldn't cash his check or even open up a bank account because he lacked state issued identification. He was in a perfect catch twenty-two, he couldn't get his ID because he didn't have his birth certificate from another state, but the state couldn't issue his birth certificate without identification. Finally, the advocate had to write to a congressman, who in turn lifted the Patriot Act restrictions for this vet and issued him a temporary state ID that lasted a few months so he could get his birth certificate. When everything was finally worked out, the check was cashed, and this poor vet finally moved into his house; he died a few weeks later sleeping on his floor. He said he never quite felt comfortable sleeping on a bed.

The situation with the single mother went substantially smoother and had a happier ending. Because we were able to take her into the shelter without an ID, she was able to secure all the necessary documentation to get a driver's license and within a few weeks she had a job. Shortly after that she was able to get financed for a car and eventually moved out of the shelter within about a month and a half. Because we didn't place the burden of a time limit on her, it gave her the feeling of security. No longer worrying if her kids would be able to eat or have a safe place to sleep meant that she could focus her energy on getting them registered with the state voucher daycare program and seek employment. To this day she continues to be a successful person and a loving mother and has maintained her housing and car. She just needed an opportunity, not a bunch of rules.

The next year she came back, just like many others did, and volunteered so that others who had been in her shoes could experience the same type of quality care she did. This is the power of trusting people and being truly patient with their situation. It takes individual care to create unique and individual results for every client.

A Cheerful Giver

Being homeless is a full-time job and extremely expensive. Whenever someone tells me that they believe the homeless population must be lazy, I literally laugh in their face and offer for them to spend a day on the streets with me. No one has taken me up on the opportunity yet. I've spent an entire day walking around with one of my close friends who lives on the streets. I met him as the sun came up and we walked together everywhere—to his first meal for breakfast and then five miles up the street to the mission that would be serving lunch, and then over to the location where he had his mail sent. They also had washers and dryers so we waited until his wash was clean and then trekked back downtown toward his camp. He informed me that we had missed dinner and so we cooked some expired beans over his fireplace. This man was in far better shape than I have ever been in my entire life. One bad decision in his late teens had landed him a felony and for a long time he couldn't find anyone who would hire him. So he finally gave up trying. All of his friends growing up had joined the military but he couldn't because of an injury. Life was against him and he knew it. So he would take odd jobs when he could and then spent his day walking from one location to another just to survive.

His camp was located on a large piece of abandoned property that sat right on the edge of the bay. This location would one day be turned into a world class baseball stadium. But, for today, as it had been for decades before, it was the home of the forgotten. It was known as The Badlands.

"You know," he said to me as we looked out over the sunset, "I would do just about anything to live in a house, to have air conditioning and not have someone spit on me for being down. But I swear to God, I would miss this view every single day."

Whether you are the CEO, executive director, board member or volunteer at a non-profit or charity, it is important to remember that if you are going to achieve your maximum success, which is really the client's success, you can only truly do so by focusing on individualized care management. The people we are called to serve, our clients and friends, are as unique as that sunset I shared with him that day. Every single one is as beautiful and as changing as the seasons. When we require our clients to jump through hoops, we are oftentimes asking them to do the impossible. It's time to ask yourselves what benefits do your current rules and regulations offer? When was the last time you evaluated them and compared them to the best practices nationally? If you are a volunteer or donor, are you asking those in charge of the places you give to and work freely for these tough questions?

Often, the work that we do is compared to being a type of hospital. Most charities, when we are honest with ourselves, act more like a war zone medic running around giving morphine so that the soldier can die with dignity and just hoping that the chaplain shows up to give them last rites. We have to get out of the ER and war zone mentality and start thinking of the long-term wellness plan like a general practitioner. It isn't enough just to stuff gauze in a gaping wound. And there is no doubt that we need these first responders! But in order to truly address the long-term cures, we must begin treating the actual symptoms. And I don't mean that those experiencing homelessness, or any other client base, are the symptoms but rather that the system we have created in our society that allows for homelessness, lack of healthcare or whatever thing our charities supplement to exist at all, much less at the rate it does, is a cancer on our society that genuinely calls into question whether we should legitimately be able to call ourselves a first-world country.

But, fortunately, there is a cure. We just have to be willing to do the nearly impossible to access it: admit that we might not be doing this thing called charity right.

CHAPTER THREE

Kindness

If you haven't got any charity in your heart, you have the worst kind of heart trouble.
Bob Hope

Problems of the Heart

I got a call late one night from a friend of mine who runs a street outreach. "I don't know if I can keep doing this." He poured out his heart over the cellular waves as he shared one story after another. He was entrenched in the camps with those who were struggling for basic survival. His day-to-day was filled with meetings on the street and finding ways he could help. The struggle for him was growth because he was stretched beyond what any reasonable person could handle.

"We've got a guy out here trying to get his son back and we are hitting every roadblock imaginable," he told me.

This was the thing that was really weighing on him. He could see the system and how it was supposed to work, but this guy was falling through the cracks. The advertised promises of certain agencies weren't living up to the actual reality of this individual client's circumstance, and in the middle of all of this were a child who desperately wanted to be reunited with his father and a father who was doing everything he could to get his son back.

So I listened as this non-profit executive ripped his heart right out of his chest and left it bleeding there for the world to see. If love alone could fix a problem, then he would make this whole thing right. But the problem is you can't pay a deposit on an apartment with blood.

The business of non-profits can oftentimes take the heart and soul right out of even a very well-intentioned mission statement. Almost every charity begins out of the kindness of others who desperately want to meet a need that they see in this world. However, this can lead to two very ineffective ways of operating.

On one hand, you have the type of non-profit that lacks any sense of business acumen. Think of the bumbling executive director who is always falling over paperwork stacked in the corners; this director is typically not paid at all or severely underpaid and is always on the brink of burnout. Their deep love for the project and the clients lends toward them making unnecessary personal sacrifices. Everything seems like a life or death situation to them, mostly because everything is. One missed meeting can lead to their micro organization falling into complete ruin. Inevitably, this model falls apart at the seams as soon as the person steering the ship crashes. I can't tell you how many kindhearted people I've seen finally lose it and throw a chair during a board meeting.

The reverse narrative is, of course, the Type A personality executive who runs a tight ship but won't allow anyone to slip through who doesn't match the absolute qualifications. This person is always paid on time because they aren't going to gamble their pay check by allowing a single individual to receive any benefits from the charity that doesn't absolutely need to. All quotas are met and compassion is not part of the purpose of their organization because their purpose is to meet a particular function.

I remember clearly one of the first times I engaged with this second type of executive director. It was an alarming experience, and it certainly wouldn't be the last time I met someone who operated a non-profit this way.

There was an organization that had been founded by a number of different churches that were ideologically, albeit not theologically, aligned. They wanted a singular source to funnel their funding into where they could send people who were in need of assistance with rent and utilities. These churches felt this would limit the abuse of their benevolence funds. On the surface level, it seemed like a really good option. This way, whenever someone in need would approach a church secretary or warden, they could all give the same pat answer: "We don't distribute funds through the church. Please visit this charity instead." The problem was each church had slightly different agendas that they wanted to meet and the board was made up of members of each of these churches. They acted as watch dogs to make sure that every cent was spent, not just correctly but in line with those ideologies that were important to them. This left the director of the charity having to contort to meet this rigid criterion.

This caused everything to become so formulaic that the human element was lost in the process. I observed their routine one day and watched as mothers waited in the entry room hoping that their electric bill might be paid or at least a portion of their rent. One by one I watched as potential clients were rejected because they missed the mark by margins. One woman made $13 dollars too much per month to qualify. Just $13 dollars difference and her electricity was back on the chopping block, it was going to be a cold winter for her and her newborn. Another person was rejected because they had utilized this service in the past and was still within the window for not being able to request help again.

Volunteers carefully screened each client, first asking them to answer a series of questions on a piece of paper.

I was also handed one of these intake forms to review. It was clear that this was a copy of a copy of a copy. It had been xeroxed to death and was barely legible any longer. It was almost a metaphor for this organization. Once these forms had been filled out, an interview was conducted. Occasionally, people would be asked for supporting documentation, pay stubs or commitments from their landlords that they would in fact, not be kicked out if they did secure the funding from this group.

"I don't want my landlord to know I'm in this situation!" a single mother pleaded.

"But we have to," the volunteer urged. "Our policy clearly states your landlord has to fill out this form."

"Ma'am, I start my new job in a week. I don't want him to know I'm unemployed. Please, is there anything—"

"This is our policy."

Each person met challenges along the way trying to fit within the formula that was set before them, all written by board members who likely had never been forced to sit in a room like this, justifying their circumstance and attempting to fit their crisis within the margins. I thought of the disciples pushing away the woman with a discharge of blood. "Don't bother the master," was dripping off of every form and rule.

Finally, once a small group of people had survived the Hunger Games, their forms would be taken to the executive director as she sat behind her desk. I couldn't help but feel a bit like I was in Dolores Umbridge's office. I watched as she coldly looked over each form, sorting them and giving momentary acknowledgments of my presence by giving short, often one-word explanations for rejection:

"Income."

"Unsustainable!"

"Where's the father?"

Once the winners of the day were finally selected, many were given other tasks yet to be accomplished. What began at 7AM was now winding down well into the afternoon, with many people not being rejected until the very end. Another day wasted when these women could have been calling friends or family, promising that they really would pay them back this time or standing on street corners holding signs, hoping for the spare change of kind neighbors. Other women would have resorted to other activities to ensure that their children would not spend a night sleeping on the streets. What stood between these women and prostitution all rested in the highly pragmatic judgment calls of an admittedly cold person who cared about the numbers and not the end results.

Both of these models fail the clients in different ways. The overly loving director ultimately fails them by never seeing anything through to completion and the hyper focused and critical person never allows kindness and compassion in, lest they be taken advantage of. In order for any charity to hit the mark, it has to be both willing to be business savvy and willing to bend its own rules for the sake of decency. Even Jesus broke the Sabbath so that his disciples could eat, saying, "The Sabbath was made for man, not man for the Sabbath." In this same way, rules are made for us, but we aren't made simply to obey rules. They can be important guide posts and keep us in check.

I remember reading about a husband who was speeding to drive his wife, who was in labor, to the hospital. He broke the speed limit. He broke the rules. When he was pulled over, the officer arrested him for this and he missed the birth of his child. I don't remember hearing many people praising the officer for this decision. As a society, the majority of us acknowledge that the rules exist to keep us safe, but the second the rules no longer keep us safe, there are circumstances where we must bend the rules. As Dr. King once said, "One may well ask: 'How can you advocate breaking some laws and obeying others?'" The answer lies in the fact that there are two types of laws: just and unjust. I would be the first to advocate obeying just laws. One has not only a legal but a moral responsibility to obey just laws. Conversely, one has a moral responsibility to disobey unjust laws. I would agree with St. Augustine that, 'An unjust law is no law at all.'"

Once our rules cause us to let people starve simply because it's after sundown, we have lost sight of the purpose for which they were instituted. We don't create rules as a non-profit in order to allow a mother to lose her electricity over $13 dollars any more than the Sabbath was created so that people would be bound to their couches in misery. In both circumstances, these rules were designed to create peace for a person. Once a rule has reached a point that it prevents a client from reaching success, merely to follow the rule, we have lost sight of the total purpose of any charity.

Applying for Burnout

The reason why so many charities get stuck with less charitable directors is because the kind ones burn out before their project becomes successful. Every day, thousands of non-profits are started that never see the completion of their goal because someone takes on the task of director and never sees the fruits of their labor. So, as in any business, it is often only those who are willing to cut throats to get to the top that actually make it. Am I implying that all non-profits are filled with shady executives who only look after themselves? Certainly not! But I do think we need to be honest with ourselves about this toxic reality that exists within the industry.

How then do we begin to shift the pendulum in such a way that the kind people with soft hearts are making good decisions and at the helm of the organizations that we are entrusting with our money? The answer is extremely simple and it really falls on the volunteers and board members to have a change in mindset and a softening heart themselves.

I was putting in a bid for a consulting job for a non-profit and when the executive director received my proposal and quote, she responded with, "We simply can't afford this."

Now, keep in mind that this director had contacted me because their organization was hemorrhaging and falling apart at the seams. They had a perfectly good plan; they had followed through and received their 501c3 and were just about to get their first building. The woman who founded the organization had quit her day job and was now acting as the executive director. But she knew that there were a lot of pieces missing from the puzzle. Her initial email to me spoke of how conflicted she felt about her circumstance; she wanted to be on the streets with the people she was called to serve, not stuck in an office filing endless paperwork. So my first reply to her was, "You need to hire an assistant."

Her response to this was the same as her response to my consulting proposal. "I can't afford that!"

I shot her another quick email. "You aren't getting paid, are you?"

"No," was her simple reply.

"You need to be getting paid for the work you are doing!"

"We can't afford that right now."

I took a while to respond, and then I laid some truth on her. "You can't afford not to get paid. Your organization is failing because you won't invest in the things you need in order to succeed. If you don't get paid, if you don't hire an assistant, your non-profit won't exist in a year."

The problem that this director was facing is something that countless others face every single year. They are too kindhearted to acknowledge their own value. Far too often we don't appraise ourselves appropriately and we refuse to admit our own importance in the organization. The reality is most people don't see the countless hours of hard work that these directors put in, mostly because volunteers and board members are doing this work on their free time and because it is something that they enjoy. They like putting on the bake sale for their favorite charity and so, since they are having fun at the event, they assume that this feeling is mutual for the director. Not realizing, of course, that the director has been working all day on menial tasks that they never anticipated would be part of their job, and that this event is on a Saturday night, meaning they are missing their kid's dance recital, a date with their partner or any other number of things they would rather be doing other than working a 15-hour day with little or no pay.

This kind person will eventually feel so disheartened by all their free or underpaid labor that they will eventually walk away from this field feeling defeated and like a failure. On other occasions, they are fired for underperformance, not because they aren't giving their all to the clients but because they aren't succeeding in the areas they aren't good at. And, in most circumstances, they never claimed to be good at those areas in the first place. This happens all of the time. This is where the kindhearted directors go, out to pasture. It is only AFTER losing their fearless leader that boards and volunteers quickly scramble to raise enough funds to bring in someone on a competitive wage. They then bring in someone who is good at the business of charity (but not necessarily actually good at business), who is diligent at fundraising, someone completely unlike their previous director. When the success happens, they wrongfully assume that the success is brought about by the skill set that this director brings that the other director did not have. These volunteers rarely realize that the fundamental difference was not technique or skill but salary.

Before buildings and buying vans for toting around goods, before opening thrift stores, and any other thing that will make your organization "feel" like a real charity, if you are going to reach success, you have to commit to bringing in qualified staff. If, as a board and volunteers, you aren't willing to take on the commitment of hiring someone to do all the day-to-day tasks that you don't want to, then you aren't truly committed to the cause because these directors work hard. They do the jobs you wouldn't waste your time volunteering to do. They attend all the work day meetings like lunch with the big donors or the hours-long coalition meetings, board meetings, and city council meetings. If you aren't willing to take on that charge you must create a salary for this person. Yes, their work looks different than yours. But you are tasking them with a very unique job: to be the hands, feet, and voice of your organization.

Striking a Balance

Kindness and compassion should be the bench mark of any charitable work, but pragmatism does get the job done, so we often default to it. Kind people rarely keep the lights on and the water bill paid. They do tend to lean toward the client and let other things fall to the wayside. That is why it is so fundamentally important to breathe with both lungs within your charity. These shouldn't be labored breaths but rather both working in unison with each other. Because neither of these models in and of themselves is wrong. You do need people who are willing to do the boring tasks of paperwork and fundraising. However, you need it just as much as you need someone who's willing to look at a situation and say, "I know this client has been with us fourteen times in the last two years, but I know this person, and there is a genuine difference in their countenance right now. I believe they are going to make a change and I need you to trust me on this. Write the check."

One of the ways we fail at anything is trying to get people to fit into molds that they were never designed to be in. The passionate people who carry the flame of an organization are often very disorganized themselves. Think of any person throughout history who changed the world and read their biography, most of the thinkers are spoken about as being in love with their work but always late, never meeting deadlines, and often buried in paperwork that was never finished. Then there are the doers who are always half an hour early, everything is done by a schedule, and they get the job done on time or before. Both of these personalities have value and purposes. But when we allow only one of them to reign in the area of charity, we lose the heart of our calling.

We need people who are willing to hold folks accountable and make sure that the basic needs of the organization are being met. I am in no way suggesting that your organization should always be late on rent in order to pay someone else's; that is not sustainable. However, if you are never willing to take risks, you'll never know if that machine can fly or if you really can build a computer in your parents' basement. You have to be willing to make bold mistakes in order to see what the final outcome might be. Sometimes you'll fail and other times you'll succeed. It is in the experimentation phase that we really learn what we as individuals and as an organization are made of. Without risks, though, we lose out on opportunities for the miraculous to happen. Entrepreneurs who succeed in business take risks, they create partnerships with people who have different skill sets than themselves and power forward. In order for a non-profit to truly succeed, it does not need to abandon these practical principles that work within business, it needs to emulate them.

The easiest way to succeed in the area of charity is to lead with the heart and have the right hook of structure for when things are going off track. When we lead with our rules and rituals, instead of with compassion, we lose the ability for our organizations to flourish. We do need a good backbone and that is precisely why boards exist. In the last organization I worked for, my treasurer was truly my steady rock. She always kept me in line and we certainly locked horns a couple of times over deadlines and the need for her to bend on occasion and trust me. But it was also for me to learn the value of staying on task so we wouldn't miss important grant proposals. However, at the end of the day she kept me in line and I forced her to look for gray areas stuck in between the tight numbers and fractions in her brain. That water and oil, yin and yang approach maintained a very important balance within our organization. We never overspent and we always stayed within the margins, but we also never said no to someone if it was truly important.

This is why it is essential to have a balance of power. No one person should have godlike authority within your organization. This creates a dangerous imbalance. No matter what your title might be, everyone should have someone they have to ask permission from. This creates an environment where everyone feels like there are checks and balances. This also gives donors a feeling that they aren't just writing checks that are being eaten up by overheads. It almost seems ironic that it is when we take the time to pay people right and invest in our projects properly that we are able to make a real commitment to our donors that their money is being spent wisely. That's because our charity runs most effectively when we place people in charge who have a heart for it, and then we supplement their inabilities instead of demanding that they be everything to everyone. If your director isn't good at keeping the books, it's better to hire an accountant than it is to fire a good director and hire someone who is rigid but good with Quicken.

The practicality of all of this is found in the core question we must ask ourselves: how can we expect our clients to rise above poverty if our organizations operate within the same desperate cycles that our clients do? We don't want our clients to be worried about where their next meal is coming from or if they will be able to keep their electricity on, so why do we expect that for our executive directors or even the program itself? We wouldn't want our guests to have to beg on the street for spare change, but we expect our directors to literally have to beg for donations just to survive. In order to properly help our clients, we must be the example and not kindred spirits both fighting to survive.

No business can survive if they are spending more than they make. They have to have balanced practices and portfolios. You must plan for the future, not spending yourself to the max every year hoping that your fund-raising cycle next fiscal year will be the same as the year previous. That doesn't work because you have to build upon the reality that crashes will come, emergencies will happen, and unpredictable weather can strike at any moment. Non-profits rarely build nest eggs or prepare for marketplace loss. No matter what demographic you serve, teaching clients about how to properly manage their plans, finances, and schedules exists within nearly every field of the non-profit sector. Unfortunately, this is almost always done hypocritically with, "Those who can't do, teach," firmly pressing tongue in cheek.

This means that we have to make different choices than our clients are making. We have to stop thinking about basic survival and instead look toward future success. Sometimes that means we have to hire real plumbers to fix an issue, bring on a full-time accountant, hire a consultant to help us look for blindspots and failures within our organization. If no one in your organization is proficient in grant writing, hire someone. If you don't know how to do social media marketing, bring in someone who does. If you do these things correctly, just like with any business, those new positions will pay for themselves within the first fiscal year and generate a profit within the second fiscal year. When we are willing to take those risks and invest back into these programs we love, its then that we are able to position ourselves to allow directors and staff to say yes when they need to because we are following a model that's looking towards success.

We are like the parent who takes the time to model a good relationship for our children in hopes that they will emulate. So, for the sake of our clients, we have to be the good parent who both sits at the kitchen table balancing the check book in front of our kids while also being willing to stop halfway through to go play ball.

CHAPTER FOUR

Not Envious

Every man must decide whether he will walk in the light of creative altruism or in the darkness of destructive selfishness.
Martin Luther King Jr.

Myths and Legends

Speaking in hyperbolic terms, there are two major demographics that care about a cause: non-profits and activists. There exists almost a relative culture war between these two groups. Non-profits, in many senses, look at activists as being ideologues who are only bothered with disruption, while the non-profits see themselves as busy doing the real work. In many ways, the activists have a similarly disparaging opinion of non-profits. They view them as money sucks that are disembodied from the reality and plight of those in need of help. This contempt creates a vacuum where very little can be accomplished. I have been on both sides of these ideological fences and the reality is that there is validity to both arguments, though each side would begrudge me for saying so. Non-profit executives rarely want to face the reality of how the corporate nature of many of these organizations prohibits them from certain levels of care. In equal measure, many activists don't want to admit the value that some of these non-profits bring to the table.

The reality is that much of the issue lies in envy on both sides. Whenever I have been on picket lines or during food distributions with my activist friends, their complaints are legitimate. They are providing services for pennies on the dollar. They will lament what they could accomplish with six or seven-figure budgets. They see wasteful spending all around and often balk at executives' salaries. However, many of these rogue organizations end up bleeding to death because burnout inevitably comes when you are providing a free service and are not being paid for your hard work and dedication. Once someone walks over the picket line into the non-profit sector, they are treated with bitterness by their fellow activists. I've felt that sting a few times myself, both as someone who has watched my friends do something that I perceived as "selling out" and as the person being accused of selling out. Activists are also treated with contempt by the establishment.

I remember an interview one such activist turned non-profit executive director gave to a morning show. At the end of a thorough and thought-provoking interview, the host said, "Well, later today we will be having the professionals on to discuss this as well." How much more of a professional did this person need to be in order to be considered equally an expert on the subject?

The flip side to all of this is that non-profits feel a sense of bitterness and envy towards those involved in activism. They feel as if there is a level of advocacy to the work they are accomplishing. They view the activist as a person who is able to float through life with little to no rules or consequences to their actions. They aren't concerned with budgets and board meetings and the daily struggles of keeping an organization afloat. In their minds it is easy for an activist to criticize the hard work they are doing when they simply prepare a meal a few times a week. Even though it can be a frustrating experience and it is easy to fall into the trap of discrediting them or even looking at those who question us as the opposition, it is important instead to look at those who call us to the table as a form of accountability. If what we are doing has merit and purpose, the questions will fall away by the example of the work. Otherwise, it might be time to take a step back and instead realize that we might just need a little activism. It might be time to even protest ourselves a little bit.

Both groups carry a very important mantle and need validation for their efforts. Our community non-profits do provide important services. Likewise, our activists do as well. The truth of the matter is that most communities do not have enough available services to meet all the needs of those they are intended to serve. Without the supplementation of these smaller rogue groups providing food, clothing, and other essential needs, many people would go without daily necessities like food and water.

The real danger is when this battle of ideologies creates such bitterness that these two lungs of service stop breathing together and we choke out.

Many years ago, I attended a local homeless coalition meeting with a number of activists to discuss the dangers that cold weather presented for our area residents experiencing homeless. The director of the coalition at the time disputed many of our concerns. This small group of activists was not simply comprised of supposed "extremist types" (not that it should matter); our group was compromised of a local college professor, some of his students, a few aging hippies, and myself, a young idealistic priest. Our major concerns were that many of the shelters had rules that were prohibitive to some of those who were most vulnerable to the elements: people who lacked proper identification or suffered from substance abuse disorders. The logic at the time was that those who might appear to be under the influence of drugs or alcohol would be turned away at the door so they wouldn't pose a threat to the general shelter population. However, these people were at the greatest risk of exposure, hypothermia, and death. Toward the end of our civil discussion, the idea began to float around about conducting some sort of march or demonstration to create awareness about our concerns. We asked for the support of the homeless coalition to help raise that awareness.

"This is not the type of advocacy that the coalition would like to participate in," the director told us.

"This is exactly the type of thing we should participate in," I quickly responded. "At the end of his life, this was specifically the call Dr. King was sending out, to raise awareness of the plight of the poor and homeless."

"Well," the director said with a cold and determined look on his face, "Dr. King and I do not see eye to eye on that method."

The director began to regurgitate a common, but false, narrative about homelessness; he accepted that the majority of those suffering on the streets were there by choice. He even challenged those in attendance by saying that he had hundreds of vouchers for homeless veterans that would expire soon and that none of those staying on the streets had ever attempted to qualify for this program. He informed us that, at any given moment, if a veteran wanted off the street, all he would have to do was ask but, according to the director, no one was asking. With this, the coalition director wrongly believed that none of those staying on the streets or holding signs begging for money were in fact homeless. This is a common falsehood that often circulates concerning those living on the streets.

The professor stood up from the table in clear frustration. "Well, sir, have you even bothered to go into any of the encampments to see if there are veterans there?" And with that the good doctor turned and left.

Later that week, the professor challenged that director on his promise. He brought a veteran to one of the public meetings and asked if he could get into housing. As it turns out, the voucher system wasn't as easy as the director had let on. But that in-person confrontation, with a real-life person in need of help, began to change the conversation. It turns out that this little bit of activism was necessary, albeit uncomfortable, in order to bring about real change.

The core issue at play here is one of marketing. Many times those of us in the non-profit sector have a, "if you build, they will come" mentality. As cute as the marketing strategy might be for a film, it doesn't work in practicality. As a matter of fact, I worked out of the office of a baseball park for a while. It may have been a field of dreams but, in reality, there was a great deal of marketing that went on behind the scenes to make sure that "they would come". I saw the level of marketing and strategy that went into each and every move they made. Sure, it seemed effortless to the general public, but, in reality, everyone from the team owner all the way to the janitor worked in unique ways to promote their efforts. Promotion is something we often fail at within our industry and yet activists excel at.

I've seen hundreds of people rally to a cause in a matter of hours because passionate folks sent out a rallying cry. Change comes through passion and passion can be a messy business. Bleeding hearts will leave bloodstains on the carpet. In business, we wear our blood, sweat, and tears as badges of honor. If you take the time to listen to anyone who has succeeded in entrepreneurship, they brag about the long hours they had to put in to build their empires. Those stripes are their pride and joy because it was though that hard work, the give and the ask, that they accomplished their success.

Activism gives a level of gratification that collating budget requests in a stuffy office can't. But both are important. We have failed within the non-profit industry at tapping into the heart of the salt of the earth folks who make the world turn. We have falsely begun to believe that in order for our organizations to thrive we must be clean cut and narrow, divorcing ourselves from the grit and reality of what is at stake. I'll guarantee you it's more difficult, but the rewards are greater.

Instead of it being a fight of, "We have vouchers," and rebuttals of, "I'll show you because I actually know the folks on the street!" there was a lost marketing opportunity of cross pollination. These two worlds shouldn't be at odds with each other, they are harmonious—but only if we will allow it.

If you assume that because your organization's phone lines are constantly busy with people making the ask you must be reaching everyone in need, you are fooling yourselves. I would argue that you might not even be coming close to touching the tip of the iceberg and it's even more likely you aren't accessing the clients in most need of help. You are missing the cancer patient who is slowly dying, afraid and alone, in their home. But you know who has access to that person? The activist who spends every Tuesday afternoon bringing them a meal. If you want to change the entire operation of how you do business and maximize your success, find ways to create inroads, and even paid positions, for those whom you consider to be on the fringe. Because you know who the clients are calling after your doors close at 4:59? An activist.

Shell Shock

Within our society there exists a cold war on the narrative of poverty and homelessness. A type of smear campaign that is used to justify away guilt in exchange for displacing responsibility off of those of us who are charged with addressing these issues and onto the client. With hushed whispers, stories are told about panhandlers who actually drive a Mercedes or that one single mom who intentionally misleads charities in order to have her electric bill paid over and over again. The rumors move and circulate without anyone knowing who the original culprits are or what town these mythologies originated in. Whenever these stories have been relayed back to me, it's always someone's cousin or best friend's friend who definitely witnessed these events. How magical that these stories all share similar narratives and characters, always take place in their town, and yet those of us who have worked on the forefronts haven't run across the shady individuals duping the system.

Herein lies the frustration that many activists feel; that many non-profits have lost the desire to advocate on behalf of their clients and share the realities that they face in their daily lives. Now, am I denying that there are people who game the system? No, I am certainly not going to say it has never happened. The issue here is that whatever instances that do exist are such a dramatic minority that these stereotypes need to be put to rest because the damage that they do to our clients is real and dramatic. We have to lay these tall tales to rest once and for all; we have to lead with the narrative of hope and success.

I remember a night one of our volunteers at the shelter had to cancel last minute due to an illness and so I had to step in. I had already worked a full day of being bothered with the tedious and boring part of being an executive director— the paperwork, returning telephone calls, emails, and lunch meetings that always run over time. I was exhausted and all I wanted in the world was to be home with my family. When I walked in through the door to relieve the first shift volunteer, they were eager to bounce out the door.

I lay down on the couch in the common room and pulled my paperboy hat over my eyes, already dreading the 5 AM wakeup call of the elderly woman who made the coffee in the morning. Most people drink coffee, she chewed it. I was not the only person who had noticed this. She would wake up at the exact same time every morning, brew a pot of coffee and proceed to make this weird chewing sound that eventually turned into her making another noise, a guttural moaning sound that resembled what one might make after taking the first bite of a gourmet meal. And this happened. Every. Single. Morning.

No sooner had I closed my eyes and begun to drift off to sleep than I heard a soft voice. "Nate." I darted back to reality and titled my hat upward and saw the blurry outline of one of the mothers who was staying with us.

"Yes? Are you okay?"

"No, I am not okay."

It was a stupid question for me to ask, it was genuinely rhetorical. I could hear in her voice that something wasn't alright. She sounded almost like my own mother when she is holding back tears. It brought back memories of my childhood and those moments when my parents were confronted with the reality of their own poverty and homelessness. These moments always grabbed me by the throat and dragged me back, sitting there in the back seat of our minivan/home, listening to my mother's cries. On those long nights of uncertainty in my youth, I could not sleep but I also couldn't do anything to change anything about our circumstance. In these moments, when I was equally unable to sleep, I had a different stature because I did have the ability to make a difference in these circumstances. I couldn't be there for my own mother in the ways I wished I could, but through the redemptive work I was now able to do, I could change the ending. I now had the power. So with that realization always at the forefront of my mind, I sat up and refocused my vision. This wasn't my mother, but she was someone's mother, and in the other room there were kids who weren't me. Just the same, our stories crossed paths and they were not the tales of myths about poverty but the gross reality of it.

"I was at the store," she began, "and someone started making fun of me for having a phone while using my food stamp card. It hurt me so deeply. I have to have my phone so that, when work calls, I know my schedule. Sometimes they call me in last minute. But now I don't want to even take my phone in public."

Yes, I had witnessed this firsthand as a child. I had experienced this very same prejudice and watched as my mother was humiliated numerous times while out shopping with me and my siblings. People felt genuinely entitled to express their views on our current plight. They felt no shame in telling us which luxuries in life they felt our family was undeserving of. And here was this woman going through this exact same pain. I watched as her children played with toys on the ground of the common room, knowing all too well that their little ears were being filled with these stories and that they would be memories they would carry with them for the rest of their lives. It would taint their view of their fellow human beings and the world around them. It would shape their opinions on religion, politics, and society as a whole. Most importantly, it would shape how they felt about themselves and their parents. I know because I lived it as a child. For decades we've allowed these stereotypes to exist and then it empowers folks to be cruel to people they've never met, people like my mother, this mother, and countless other mothers and fathers who are doing the best they can within our broken system of survival.

I also knew how I responded would matter because, just as much as those biting moments of cruelty stuck deep within my soul, it was in the kindness of others, in their generosity, that I found my purpose and calling. I saw in them the man I wanted to grow up to be, someone who would fight until my knuckles were raw. We are given a great power because we are all that stands in between people and their hopes. Every acceptance of a person can change their life but so does every rejection. And depending on what area of service we provide, it can literally be the difference between life and death. So this power is something we should never take lightly and must acknowledge with great humility.

More important than what I would say in this moment would be how I would respond with palpable action. Reassuring words and promises are only more darkness if they are not meant with real change. But what can I alone do if she and I both are fighting against and within a broken system? I made the only promises I could muster, that I would do something. Little did I know that it would be more than just attempting to relieve her momentary suffering but also attempting to actively fight to change the very thought processes and powers attempting to hold her back from success. Thankfully, it is not a battle I have been fighting alone. You who are reading this now, and countless others, as alone as we may feel, have been fighting and sojourning together in the fields of restoration and justice.

The problem is that, in many ways, though we would hate to admit it (and many probably will actively deny it), non-profits are reliant on these stereotypes. Maybe rely is too harsh a word, though likely fitting, but they certainly benefit from them. We take checks laced with judgment and words like, "Hopefully this won't go to those scammers." Instead of speaking up, silence remains because we think we need those checks. So advocacy goes out the door for the sake of survival again. And this is where the activists come in. Whatever they lack in structure, stability, and income they make up for in shoving the reality of injustice in our faces.

Not only do we need both the advocates and the social service system but we need them to meld into a perfect union, no longer fighting against each other but acting as one stream forming together as the river of justice slowly etching away at the mountains of lies that have circulated for decades, binding and holding captive those whom we are called to serve.

Green with Envy

One day, I saw my friend Phil standing on the side of the road holding his "Will Paint for Food" sign. Phil was not traditionally homeless but always on the edge. He did have a home, if you could call it that. The little shack he rented did not having running water or heat, and the electric was rarely ever on. The slum lord he rented from refused to make common repairs to the A/C system or procure proper plumbing. He justified this because Phil was constantly running weeks and sometimes months behind on his rent. The landlord never wanted to kick him out because, one way or another, Phil always found a way to pay and the owner of the property knew that no other tenant would put up with these abuses. So this toxic landlord/tenant relationship went on for years.

Every few days, Phil would walk up to the top of the hill and hold a sign, not begging for money but begging for work. Once or twice a week, someone would stop and offer him a job painting an old garage or a new addition to their house. Most times he would work well under his value, just to be able to throw money into the never-ending pit of his perpetual debt to his slum lord. Every once in a while he would put in the hours and then people wouldn't pay him, assuming they could get away with it since who was going to advocate for a part-time drunk who full-time panhandled for jobs?

Many people wouldn't even take the time to read Phil's sign or maybe they didn't believe he really wanted work but felt sympathy for him anyway and they would reach their hand out the window and offer him a few dollars.

"I hate taking that money, Nate! I hate it. I don't want no damn handouts. But how am I going to tell them no? I want to work, but I need the money whichever which ways I get it."

I remember at one of our first meetings he told me that when he originally came out here to hold his sign, he left within thirty minutes. The next day, when he came back, he went and got a couple of beers. "Just to take the edge off, man. The things people say, I couldn't hear it sober." Phil wasn't an alcoholic but he was quickly becoming a drunk in order to numb the pain of this cruel world he was living in. He was not a stereotype but was becoming one by virtue of circumstance.

While standing there that day with him, a man pulled up and yelled something from the safety of his vehicle. "I wish that I could just quit my job and have people give me money! That would be the life. I wouldn't have to worry about anything."

In that moment I really believed that man. I think he was telling the truth, even though he said it with biting cruelty. It wasn't the first time I had heard someone say something similar about those experiencing homelessness or poverty. They remark under their breath that they wish they could camp out by the waterfront or they wish that someone else would pay their bills or that the government would buy them food. It became clear to me over time that there is a segment of society that is actually envious of those who are homeless. They do wish that they could sit on the beach and drink beer. They actually are jealous of the folks who are suffering because they assume, wrongly, that these folks are lazy and aren't working hard every day just to survive. It seems both people wish to escape into each other's lives.

What that man did not realize is that Phil's life was not easy. His wife suffered from mental illness and his home life was emotionally far more destroyed than the physical attributes of the structure he lived in. Every day Phil would make the mile-long walk back to his house, he would walk first up the hill a bit further and purchase a few essential items for his household and then he would buy one small bag of cat food. He would then slowly make his way back down the hill, feeding the stray cats along the way as he went. Phil's life was both simple and complicated. He lived forever with the stigma he was now being branded with, as a beggar, a useless person worthy of being screamed at. And so he would drink, he would drink to remember his misery no more. But that misery was still very much there in the morning to greet him with every sunrise as he made his walk of shame back up that hill.

Phil needed both an advocate and tangible help. The problem for him was that he fell through the cracks of the system; he wasn't homeless yet, he didn't have children, and yet he was begging. Oftentimes we hear stories about the beggars who go back to their home, and you know what, Phil was exactly that. So if someone told a story about how they saw him begging and they followed him, they would have seen him walk into a house. But they wouldn't be seeing the full story, not even a little bit. They wouldn't have seen the broken toilet that I once used, the one you had to take the lid off of and fill with water that escaped from the busted pipe under the kitchen sink just to be able to flush. They wouldn't have seen the hole in the living room that you had to avoid or that there was no food in the cabinets. They would have just seen a man begging and walking into a house. The reality is more difficult and nuanced, it's harder to tell and it takes diligence to educate the public on the realities our clients face every single day.

There was a young guy panhandling in the rain. I stopped to see if he needed anything. He told me that his shoes were worn through and that the water was seeping in through the soles. This was causing a number of problems for his feet and he could never keep his socks dry. That was an easy enough fix. He normally stood on a street corner that I often passed on my way into work. After supplying him with some brand-new shoes, I was excited to see him later that week. As I pulled up, I noticed he had the same old ragged shoes back on his feet. I quickly pulled over.

"Did someone steal your shoes?"

"No, man, I've still got them. It's just ... well ... people kept asking me why I was begging if I had such nice shoes on."

What my dear friend here exemplified is the fundamental problem with how our culture sees poverty and homelessness. When some of his needs were being met, he was no longer fitting within the mold that society needed him to in order to be qualified as "homeless". So, instead, he had to risk his own health and comfort to fit into that stereotypical image in order to beg for survival. This is something that we all, collectively as a society, should feel ashamed of. Through our prejudice, we force people to play the part in order to be worthy of our help.

This is why we need to work so tirelessly to break down these stereotypes and create genuine awareness. We have to stop fighting against the activists and instead we have to align with that freedom of expression and tell the truth. For every rare case of someone who attempts to take advantage, there are literally hundreds of thousands of people who are in true need of genuine help and are simply struggling emotionally, physically, and financially. And one of their greatest obstacles is overcoming the way that the world sees them. So it is now incumbent upon us to tell their real stories, even if that means it doesn't always appease the ideologies of our donors and benefactors.

If we don't make this change in operation, we deserve every single picket line that comes our way.

CHAPTER FIVE

Not Insistent

Charity is not a substitute for justice withheld.
Saint Augustine

Ba! Humbug

When the average person hears the word "homeless", it brings to mind a particular kind of imagery. The majority of folks are instantly drawn to the figure in their thoughts of the tattered beggar standing on the side of the road in stained army fatigues holding a sign asking for food or money. Though those that panhandle make up the most visible aspect of homelessness, they certainly do not make up the largest demographic of those struggling under that damning word. However, most of our municipal codes and community resources go to address this one particular demographic of people. Though this grouping of folks definitely need services, the ideology of why they're our central focus is highly skewed and in many ways problematic.

After nearly a decade-long fight against my own home town for creating an anti-panhandling ordinance, they finally had twisted and converted the language to such a fine point that it became increasingly more difficult to fight in the courts. Many activists and other concerned citizens watched in horror as the first round of anti-homeless ordinances passed the Board of County Commissioners. Shortly after this, a series of sweeps of those holding signs began to take place. First, warnings were given out and then, over the coming weeks, there were sheriff's deputies on nearly every corner ID'ing, questioning, and eventually arresting those begging for survival.

One day, I pulled the records of those who had been arrested under the new ordinance after the first year of its implementation. The number was somewhere in the low 70s and many of these arrests were of repeat offenders. Most of these folks who suffered arrest were single people living in the nearby woods in small community encampments.

Part of the outrage that those who supported these ordinances felt was that these individuals were blatantly refusing assistance offered to them in the community. Many of them almost echoed the words of Ebenezer Scrooge: "Are there no prisons? Are there no workhouses? Or if they would rather die than go there, they had better do it, and decrease the surplus population!" The prevalent belief was that there existed plenty of safety nets and that those who made "the choice" to beg, rather than benefit from these services, must be either lazy, scammers or unwilling to abide by the rules of the system. Again, we see the blame of the failure of the system fell upon the client and not upon the system that was neither being honest about the available services in our community nor what rules and limitations they actually placed upon the clients—limitations that became prohibitive to many people.

And why would these service providers tell the whole truth? Again, they are trapped in their own set of rules and limitations. If they admitted to the general public how few people they are really able to serve, the backlash would be immense. They are reliant upon donations and people shopping in their thrift stores in order to be able to serve the few that they are able. So what is a little white lie or omission for the greater good? So, in this way, those in my community, just like in your own, walk around completely unaware of the dramatic limitations that exist for those who are living on the streets.

Far too often, our industry places emphasis and even prioritization on who we believe is most deserving. Slowly we've allowed moral judgments to become industry standard. We pass on clients that are considered problem children, whether it's for housing, receiving medical treatment or any range of care that we might provide. The biggest problem with this system of selection is that it doesn't make the problem go away. Rejecting a client simply because you think they are undeserving is the professional equivalent of a child closing their eyes or covering their ears to ignore their parent. Sure, it temporally makes it so you don't see the problem, but it doesn't make the problem go away.

People are going to makes mistakes and they will mess up. Zero percent of us are perfect and when we create a system that requires perfection out of people, the organization will fail. Will it help some people some of the time? Sure. But what we have to take into consideration is that, in most cases, those of us who are gate keepers of resources like medical care, housing or food have the power to give life or take it.

I was meeting once with an executive director who brought me on to do a culture restructuring at their organization. They realized that they had gone too far with their rules and regulations. But now the new director was up against a staff that was unwilling to be compliant. They liked the old system because it was what they knew. One staff member in particular wasn't willing to budge on the issue.

"We have a responsibility to focus on people who will succeed. We shouldn't pour limited resources into someone we know will fail."

I could feel all the eyes looking at me, this was do or die and that realization is what spawned my rebuttal. "So are you willing to shoot them?"

"Excuse me?"

"Well, your program offers lifesaving resources to the community. So I'm just curious if you'd be willing to just shoot the ones that you are deciding to turn away?"

There was an instant uneasiness in the room. It's easy to distance ourselves behind our rules. People walk out of the office and never return, the truth being they might not have returned simply because they are no longer here. They didn't make it because they fell further into their opioid addiction or weren't able to find someone who would take on their cancer treatment or died under an overpass somewhere, never finding housing. We do pull the trigger, we just do it behind a desk and instead of a bullet we use bullet points on a rules list that is more about marketing than it is providing care to the client. So here is the tough truth; if you don't believe in your clients, you are probably in the wrong business and if your rules are entirely set up around the assumption that everyone is guilty, you should likely pack up shop.

My Way or (Sleep under) the Highway

My friend Tony was constantly in and out of jail, arrested time and again because he begged for change outside of gas stations. Tony was a kind and sweet man, unless you mistakenly triggered his memories of the war. If a car door slammed and sounded like gunfire, suddenly this bright and beautiful man would transition into a scared teenager on the battlefield of Vietnam. His eyes would shift from soft and glowing to darting about, looking for cover.

Sometimes he would become violent during these PTSD attacks and then he would be arrested for his outbursts. But what was his crime? Never being able to come home from a war that we forced him to fight? Tony was one of thousands of impoverished young men all over our nation who were drafted or coerced to enlist in Vietnam because they quite literally had no other future—at least that is what society had taught them to believe. Tony was one of the "lucky ones" who didn't come home in a body bag. Instead he carried the bodies of his fallen brothers around in his mind forever, constantly watching them die in an endless loop of war that played in his mind anytime a firework went off or someone accidentally dropped a mop in the shelter.

I first met this dear man during an unseasonably cold winter night for Florida. The temperatures had dropped so fast and dramatically that it rocked our entire town. As warnings went out about needing to properly cover pipes and bring your animals inside, all my mind could think about was how there were human beings sleeping outside that were in just as much danger of exposure as our pets. But no warnings went out reminding us to bring our brothers and sisters in from the cold. What a dramatic juxtaposition this presented that our fellow humans are damned to sleep outside and society faces no consequences for this, but if we did this to a dog we could be arrested for animal cruelty. Not that I am saying that a person shouldn't face consequences for doing such an inhumane thing to an animal, but rather how much more should we be held accountable as a society for doing it to our fellow human beings!

Our church collected blankets and drove around for hours passing out whatever we could to whomever we were able to find. And I found Tony. He lay against a gas station, hiding between an old phone booth and a trash can. His body shivered under the oppressive cold. He looked up at me with a sense of hope as I leaned down holding a thermal sleeping bag in my hands.

"I can have this?" he asked with nearly frozen tears in his eyes.

"Yes, but I will also take you to the mission if you would like."

"Nah, sir, I can't go to the mission. I was banned from the mission. I don't want to go back there no more even if I could. I can't handle the noise. All those voices and the snoring and the men screaming in their sleep, it just takes me back and when I go back, sometimes things don't go too well."

I later learned that what he was referring to when he said, "going back," was the war. Tony liked to be near downtown with the exception of 4th of July and New Year's, when he would spend the day trekking as far away from town as possible. But even then, in the seclusion of the woods, he could still hear the rumbles of fireworks in the distance and it would drag him back, back to war, back to holding his bleeding friends on the battlefield. It would drag him straight back to Hell. Because of this, Tony couldn't stay in the mission and so he would beg and then be arrested. Multiple thirty-day stays in the county jail each year (and at great expense to the taxpayers) all because he was one of many people unwelcome at the mission because of his limitations.

What most people in our community did not realize is that even if Tony, or the countless others, did go to the mission, they could only stay there for three nights a month. The only way to stay at the mission longer was if you were accepted into their drug or alcohol rehabilitation program. One night, I remember sitting outside of the mission with a large group of men smoking cigarettes they had found on the ground as they roamed the streets waiting for the midday check-in process to begin. An older man sitting there told me that he was in the drug program. "Are you clean now?" I asked him.

"I wasn't ever dirty to begin with." He chuckled, with rings of smoke bursting out between his broken teeth. "No sir, I had never done drugs a day in my life, but I snorted my first line of cocaine just to fail the drug test so I could get in."

The truth is I can't tell you if Tony did drugs or if he would have qualified for the additional programming that existed. What I do know is that, even if he did, he wouldn't have made it through, not because of a lack of desire but rather ability. He was limited by his own mind that had been wounded fighting for what he believed were his rights and yours. Instead of being welcomed home, he was sent to live on the streets. He, like so many others, was up against a system that was against him, not for him. He didn't fit the cookie cutter mold and so he slept outside, in the cold, in the rain, in the heat, and always on the verge of sudden death, just like he did in Vietnam. He went from fighting one war overseas to fighting an entirely different war at home.

The Real Professional Panhandlers

Whenever people walk past a homeless man begging on the side of the street, they rarely imagine his real story. They don't psychically see into the heart of someone like Tony and realize his pain. Rather, many folks impose upon this beggar a sense of wrongdoing and just assume that they could, at any moment if they desired, seek help and immediately be restored to public life as an active citizen. I've had countless people, folks that I would consider generally good people, tell me this very narrative countless times.

And can we really begrudge the non-profits for not advertising how limited their services are? What benefit would it serve a mission to put up a billboard that says the following? "Donate to the Mission: Where people can only stay three days a month because that's the best we can do with our limited resources and limitations put on us by some folks who don't understand what we, or our clients, are up against." That's just not very catchy, is it? And I doubt very many people would be scrambling to drop off their used couches at the thrift stores if they knew this information. But how did we get here? I knew the man who started this mission. He had been a friend of our family for decades. My grandfather helped put in the A/C system at their first building and my mother worked at the very first thrift store. This family had loved the community and opened this outreach program out of genuine care and concern for their fellow man and their personal desire to follow the example of Jesus. What has shifted that brought this program from functionally helping people to being a system of rules and regulations that limits its ability to serve the way that many of the staff desire to and the clients so desperately need?

The answer is not an easy one to swallow but, as the old adage goes, "the truth hurts." Non-profits are beholden to the generosity of others, not unlike the panhandler begging for spare change on the side of the road for survival. Non-profits have become corporate panhandlers begging for their brothers and sisters in hopes that they will no longer have to beg. But with this system comes a very dangerous loss of power. Donors come with their own experiences, opinions and beliefs, and if those beliefs are misguided they can shape and form how an entire organization moves forward.

Now, I am not saying that the average donor to an organization has ill will or a desire to corrupt. Rather, what I am very explicitly saying is that, over time, donors or other people in power will begin to chisel away at what works in lieu of what makes logical sense to them, regardless of its actual basis in reality. The truth remains that time limits on shelter programs have been proven to be ineffective and damaging to the client. What can a person possibly accomplish in three days to a week at a shelter that will improve their situation? Can a social worker really help them get permanent housing and employment and help clean up a dusty criminal record in a matter of 72 hours? I can assure you it's nearly impossible, outside of the miraculous.

Just as the panhandler must stand on the side of the street and listen to whatever cruelty is thrown at them and smile for sake of a few dollars, executives and boards of non-profits are subjected to listening to ideas from donors, benefactors, and even future board members that they know are ineffective. But when a million-dollar donation or grant hinges on you stepping in line just a little bit, your mind will play funny tricks on you that yielding a little is better for the many, even if it is not beneficial for the few. In this we have now betrayed the best practices for practicality and the ability to continue—in other words, survival.

This becomes one of the most dangerous aspects of the entire equation in the world of charity, as one non-profit cuts off its foot in order to save the leg another non-profit will pop up in its place. Soon there are dozens and sometimes even hundreds of non-profits competing in a community, all believing they are the one "doing the most good." They're all competing for the same handful of dollars and if there is a donor who wants to shift the way operations work, they can and will by peddling those checks from one unwilling organization to the next that might be more inclined to yield.

None of this is to say that the average benefactor has evil intentions; that's the furthest thing from the truth. However, it doesn't take a lot of misguided ideologies to plague an entire organization; it just takes one bad idea and a check with a lot of zeros.

We have to change the culture that puts power and control in the hands of those who would use stigmatizing beliefs about our clients and instead listen to those who see the day-to-day reality. Countless times over the years I've heard from executive directors and their staff as they lament government regulations and donation stipulations that don't fit the actual needs and are instead written based upon presumptions. In order to change that culture, we have to create within our own culture as non-profits a system of brutal honesty. We have to be willing to advocate on behalf of our clients, to refuse accepting the limitations and instead say, "We need a better deal." In other words, we've got to treat these exchanges the way that business people do with their investors. We have to push and fight for the best deal, not just clamber for whatever we can get.

Now we come to the real controversy that we must face, has this entire system become so ineffective that it is no longer necessary at all? The time for restructuring the entire system has come and this means that we have to re-evaluate everything that we are doing. We have to be willing to look at the best practices that are being used nationwide and realize that this means that some of our sacred non-profits are no longer reverent or necessary. We do not need competing food banks fighting each other for donations but rather centralized services that are focusing people back toward full-time housing and stability. Charity should not be used as a marketing tool to attract people to your church or organization. If you have the best interests of people in mind, then you need to get behind what works and not keep repeating broken models.

Just as we need to stop being overly insistent upon our clients, bogging them down with rules no one can keep, we have to begin to shun giving that forces our organizations to do the same. This seems counterproductive to some. "How will we survive?" But my statement of reply is always the same: "If someone's giving is changing the nature and character of your mission statement, then you aren't surviving."

We have to educate the community on the realities of our organizations, our central focuses, and best practices. If someone places stipulations on their giving, be it an individual, corporate sponsor or government agency, then it's time to put on your teaching hat and get to work making sure they understand the "why" and "how" of what you do. If they cannot get behind it, you walk way because it is better to walk away from a bad deal than to be stuck in an agreement that prevents you from doing what you really need to do for your clients.

Now, I'll preface all this to say that I'm not talking about reasonable regulations or oversight. This is not me justifying that there shouldn't be certain stipulations to grants, such as they can be only used for housing or to build a medical facility. What I am talking about is when they demand that you don't allow fathers to stay with their families or if they say you can't treat people at your free clinic if they have AIDS. That is when you fight and, if necessary, you walk away.

Business folks who succeed know when to walk away from a bad deal. You don't give away the farm. Sometimes investors will attempt to change the culture or nature of business startups too. A shrewd business person will know that it's not in their best interest to agree to something that takes them totally off path. Sure, that sometimes means they have to start back at zero. You might have to do the same. But if you truly believe in the work you are doing, you will be willing to work and fight for the right donors, the right board members, and apply for the right grants. Does it take more work? Is it more time-consuming? Absolutely. But if you are building your non-profit for a particular focus, then you need to stay driven to that cause and not just chasing any dollar that comes your way. Find the cheerful givers.

CHAPTER SIX

Not Irritable

*Charity is a supreme virtue, and the great channel
through which the mercy of God is passed onto mankind.
Conrad Hilton*

Call Me, Maybe

My eyes quickly opened and closed repeatedly like the
shutter of a lens, my slumber suddenly ended by the slow
and dull hum of my phone vibrating on the other side
of the room. The hissing sound convulsed like a mad
man threatening to jump off of the cliff of my dresser. I
watched in slow motion as my phone danced closer and
closer to the edge with each buzz and then stopped. Even
though my ringer was off, it was clear that this was not
just one telephone call but a series of calls. My phone
constantly buzzed. It was always there as a never-ending
reminder of calls, texts, and unanswered emails reminding
me of all the despair in the world. Families being evicted

from their homes, mothers being replaced by "younger models" and abandoned to a cruel world. Children crying in the background as their moms pleaded their case for a room at the shelter. I knew that, once I braved the cold that awaited me outside of my comfortable bed, there was some genuine emergency on the other end of that phone. I took one more fleeting moment and imagined my phone just finally having the courage to throw itself off the dresser and smashing into a million pieces. I thought of the unending silence and lack of worry. Sure, the world would still be crashing and burning around me, but I would be oblivious, at least for a few moments. Then reason came rushing back into my brain and I ran across the room to pick up the phone. It was my late shift volunteer. By this point the shelter was already supposed to be closed down for the day and everyone out following their case management plans.

"Hello," I said half-heartedly.

"Nathan, we have an issue." I could hear screaming in the background. "There is a fight and if you don't get here soon I'm going to have to call the police."

I quickly changed into something that remotely looked suitable to wear in public and ran out the door. I lived only a mile from the shelter and so I could usually make pretty good time during an emergency. I walked into a chaotic scene that is normally only reserved for late nights at a bar or maybe Jerry Springer. Two of the women staying at the shelter were in an epic battle, with others circled around, in less than genuine tones telling them to stop, but you could see in their eyes they were eager to see who was going to actually throw the first punch. Up until this point, only food and a few of the donated clothing items had been the victims. The room was an absolute disaster as these women did their dance of spite. I walked in to people applauding, like I was the referee about to make the best call.

"I told you I would call him!" my volunteer screamed. "Now he will handle it. I told you I would call."

What was supposed to be my morning off had now become hours-long sessions, interviewing witnesses, talking to each one of the women individually, and trying to sort out the mess. Fights did not happen often at the shelter but when they did occur, it was always quite the ordeal. Even though our volunteers went through very thorough training to equip them with most problems they might face, whenever there were physical or verbal alter-cations they were always required to call me. Now, I'm not certain if it was just the universe always getting a good laugh at my expense or if it was just in my head, but it always seemed to me that these events were reserved to only happen on my day off.

I can't tell you what the fight was about, my memory fails me at this point, but what I do know is that I felt a sudden sense of frustration and despair as I looked at the minutes quickly ticking away on the clock and realized all my plans I had made for that day—grocery shopping, paying the bills, and spending time with my family—were moving further and further away from becoming a reality. I was being filled with a sense of irritability at both our guests and even the volunteer. Why couldn't this have been resolved in a civil manner? Was it really that important to get into a fight at 7:30 AM over who had the best seat or whatever asinine thing it was that started this whole scrap? Couldn't my volunteer have found some reasonable solution before things had escalated to such a volatile point? In these moments, I think it is easy for the paid staff at a non-profit to become a bit envious of our volunteers who can literally walk away at any moment. And these are the moments that burnout are made of.

The reality is, though, that this form of irritation is birthed out of a lack of compassion, even if it is only momentary and not systemic. It is easy to forget what our clients are going through and their day-to-day fears. Sure, we might be right in the thick of it with them for many hours of the day, working on their case management plans, hearing their stories, and even shouldering some of the burden for them, but the truth is that these moments of acting out really come from a place of frustration and fear. These are the times when we can either become bitter and shut off or we can push in deeper, attempting to get to the root cause of the issues.

I encourage you to push in, don't give up.

The Way Home

This probably leans into the crux of the issue from which all problems within the non-profit sector are born: irritability. It is easy to become frustrated with clients, donors, and even volunteers. This is how rules are created and regulations become cemented. One person does something wrong, or at least it is perceived as wrong, and it annoys a board member, director or volunteer. Suddenly the problem has to be addressed. Maybe the issue has even happened in a similar situation with another client and so now it has become a reoccurring issue. Meetings have to happen, solutions must be met. People start talking about real-life issues like insurance concerns. Next thing you know you are talking about policies and reform. One bad apple (or maybe two) is quite literally ruining everything for the whole batch.

Now, I'm not advocating for total anarchy here, but there does reach a certain point that our rules do become so arbitrary that they create a system that no one can navigate through or really benefit from. Just as we spoke about before, we go from having shelters that are productive and then slowly over time people are only allowed to stay for three days and next thing you know these programs are just self-perpetuating systems. So how do we find the balance between creating sensible rules that create important boundaries and recognizing that some of our regulations are not benefiting anyone at all, with the exception of isolated circumstances?

The problem with rules is that they rarely affect the people they are intended to thwart. That's why we live in a society where mothers are forced to drink their own breast milk at TSA checkpoints, yet terrorists still find a way around our checks and balances used to catch them. In a less extreme way, the protocol we create in order to stop a small number of people from "abusing the system" ends up normally harming those who genuinely need our help. That is why we have to take the time to stop and evaluate these programs and ask the tough question, "Are we actually helping the people we are called to serve in the most effective way possible?"

If we allow our frustrations with a small demographic to rule our emotions or, worse, cause us to completely approach these issues without emotions at all, then we have lost the battle of what it truly means to be a charitable people. We become a culture that is only going through the motions, like a marriage that has lost the love.

One night, I was out at dinner celebrating an anniversary and it was announced that there was another couple there celebrating one as well. They were seated a few tables away from us. I watched as they ate their meal in complete silence. The husband seldom looked up from his plate. They appeared to be in their late sixties and I'm certain that as they danced together decades ago, surrounded by flowers and family members smiling at them, they did not imagine they would be sitting here now with nothing left to say. Now, there is very little we can know about any person through casual observation, but it was hard not to wonder if the love had been lost between these two. Only my imagination could produce reasons why. However, this is not an uncommon narrative in our society.

Sometimes we continue forward, even when things aren't working, and we just go through the motions—we go on anniversary dinners, we pay the mortgage, we make sacrifices—but I can't help but wonder what the point is if we are void of the things that make life worth living. Smiles, laughter, adventure, romance. Some would argue that the importance of stability and keeping our commitments is more important than fleeting things like emotional responses. But the truth is we are emotional beings, we aren't computers. We feel pain, disappointment, happiness, and joy. It's important to rekindle these feelings and find new ways to keep those feelings alive. This is true within the context of our personal relationships. It is also true within our broader responsibility to our fellow human beings through our acts of charity.

Many non-profits have become like that couple who forgot why they got married in the first place. After decades of operation, of compromise and bending, they are just shadows of their former selves.

When I was a working as a pastor, I sat during many a marriage counseling course and rarely did those couples start these sessions out with the things they loved about each other. They would be filled with long litanies of grievances, annoyances, and irritations, both big and small. But somewhere in these folks existed the same people that fell in love, and in most cases they could and would find that love again. They had just hit a brick wall. Years of hiding emotions and over compromising had led to bitterness and pain. Once those scales were pulled away from these couples' eyes, they could address those core issues and create resolution. Slowly the romance and love could be found there, hidden behind all the pain and disappointment. They just needed an emotional baptism, a do-over.

Then there are those rare cases where couples come to the realization that maybe they had, in fact, made a mistake. There is nothing as heartbreaking as watching two adults realize that it's possible that this wasn't the path they should have chosen. Maybe some promises were broken and the damage couldn't be repaired. But they had to come to terms with the fact that their marriage had been stamped with those words that no bride or groom is thinking about as they are sailing across that dance floor: irreconcilable differences.

As difficult as it may be for some of us to accept, the truth is that if something isn't working within a non-profit, it's probably not the fault of the client but rather the organization itself. We have to stop becoming irritated with those whom we are called to serve and rather take an inward look at ourselves. If we are not producing the results we hope to see, then it's probably because we are doing it wrong. Have we in some way broken our commitments to the community? Have we become so rigid and cold in our approach that we are no longer looking at our clients with deep love and empathy? It's quite possible that for many non-profits, just like in some of the marriages I've witnessed, they have to work hard to find that purpose again. In other cases, it's time to admit that, in spite of best intentions when they started, maybe they just shouldn't have started in the first place.

Seeking Wise Counsel

We all reach points in our life where we have to face the music. Sometimes we've made bad decisions that catch up with us. Other times, circumstances beyond our control take hold and propel us into a crisis. But, at some point, we all need help and get to a point where we have to reach out for advice from others, whether it's spiritual guidance, marriage counseling or just sitting down with an old friend for advice. However, those of us who are advice givers by trade are often the last to seek counsel, even when we so desperately need it.

When I was a priest, we were required to take a pastoral retreat twice a year. During one Lenten retreat, an old monk gave a talk on the importance of confession and he exposed a reality that most of us knew but seldom talked about. Priests are the worst about going to confession. Most of us heard confession at least three times a week. Our parishioners would come and sit with us, sharing their sins, worries, and fears. They would discuss their shortcomings and hopes. We would preach about the importance of absolution and reconciliation, but few of us would take the time to go sit with our brother priests and seek our own redemption. As many of us discussed this reality after the monk gave his lecture, it became clear that these clergy weren't avoiding confession because of some delusion that they didn't need it. It wasn't as if they felt sinless, but rather it was a matter of not feeling like they had the time. It was a matter of lack of self-care. Once the door was opened and the reality was faced, the line for confession was very long that day. I guess someone just needed to say it out loud.

It fits in with the old fable of the doctor who can't keep their office plants alive. We all sort of chuckle at the notion but there is a bit of reality to it. Those who work in service fields rarely take the time to work on themselves because they are givers. But if we aren't careful, that can lead to resentment. Just like the old married couple that no longer speaks to each other, if we don't take care of ourselves and take a retreat to focus on our goals, we lose sight of who we really are.

The problem with self-care is that normally it costs money. Whether it's taking the time to go get a haircut, taking yourself out to dinner or even going on a vacation, those things are going to set you back. For non-profits, the idea of spending money that isn't on something that is considered a necessity can be a difficult task to take on. So for this reason employees normally take on tasks that they are not equipped for. Executive directors end up working eighty-hour weeks doing the jobs of three people, receptionists are required to run social media accounts, and volunteers with no experience are expected to raise thousands of dollars. But the truth is that any one of these tasks is actually a very real job and normally one that requires a particular set of tools and expertise.

An executive director asked me out to lunch one day and about halfway through our meal she cut to the chase. "We've got a real social media problem." Their non-profit wasn't staying ahead of the times and the board of directors was really putting the push on her. Other organizations of similar size had really experienced some major success getting their message out there and it was resulting in them raising some serious funds for their projects. So now her board was eyeballing her to do the same.

"I'm so frustrated," she lamented. "I don't know the first thing about running social media. It's so irritating that the board wants to put another thing on my shoulders!"

Since I was invited to this lunch, I just assumed it was to give advice, and so I offered it freely. "Have you considered hiring a media consultant? I'm sure that's how the other non-profits put together their campaigns." And it was a very clever campaign! It had everyone in town talking about the project and it even raised some controversy, in a very good way because, as they say, there's no such thing as bad press. It opened up a community discussion and though that sometimes causes lines to be drawn in the sand, it certainly opened a lot of people's eyes to the issues.

"We can't afford to hire someone to run our media right now."

Ah, yes. The never-ending paradox that we find ourselves in when it comes to effectively running a charity—

we short-change ourselves, and the people who suffer as a result are the clients.

I was running a shelter on a very tight budget and we ended up having a major plumbing issue. One of the toilets clogged the main line and put the majority of our toilets out of commission. We had five families and forty single women all using just one bathroom. We tried to avoid paying for a plumber because it was going to be expensive and so one of our volunteers mentioned that their dad had once fixed the toilet at their house. Well, that was as much expertise as we needed and so here this dad came to the rescue. After pulling out the toilet, running a snake down it and all of us battling with it for many hours, defeat was accepted. Wiping sweat from his brow, he looked up at me and said, "You might need to call a plumber."

We did, it cost money, and the problem was fixed in about thirty minutes.

The majority of us become most irritable when we are overwhelmed and then some unsuspecting (and likely undeserving) person becomes the punching bag for our frustration. If you feel like you are about to blow your lid, then it's time to release some of the steam.

Whether it's that your organization has lost its way and needs restructuring or a tune-up or you just need help with tasks that are outside of the qualifications of your staff, admitting that you need support isn't weakness, it's a powerful thing. And isn't that something we ask of our clients every single day? For our plumbing issue, had we just kept pushing through then we could have risked completely ruining the plumbing, which would have been even more costly and also led to the shelter having to close for a period of time. In this same way, if we don't take the time to invest back into our organizations, they can stagnate or close altogether. Sometimes we have to take a moment to step back and realize that businesses that do well are those that are willing to invest in their people, invest in their clients, and take risks. Even as charities, we have to take risks sometimes to push the boundaries and see what possibilities are out there.

CHAPTER SEVEN

Rejoices

When we give cheerfully and accept gratefully, everyone is blessed.
Maya Angelou

A Very, Merry Unbirthday

When I was a child, my family experienced numerous periods of homelessness and poverty. My siblings and I developed a bit of an obsession with Disney movies. These classic stories became a hiding place for our emotions. We could escape into these fairy tales where paupers became kings and soot could be turned into beautiful ball gowns. There was always a promise of hope lying out there in the future. We all held our breath waiting for a fairy godmother to come along and heal our wounds with the flick of a wrist and a bit of pixie dust.

When I was given the privilege of operating my first shelter program, it was a cold weather shelter for families with a case management program attached. It was my turn to be the fairy godparent and wave my magic wand; my turn to heal wounds, just like others had done for my family all those years ago. But I was also mindful of those who did not help, those who acted as the villains who attempted to thwart success or planted fear and doubt. One thing I learned early on in the process of working with families was that I was not unique in my love for these fables. As the kids would come into the shelter they would bring with them Woody and Buzz toys, Elsa blankets, and Mickey Mouse coloring books. This attachment wasn't just because of marketing; when you would talk with these kids, it was clear that the same things that resonated with me in my childhood were exactly the same things drawing them in as well, the hope that someone would bibbidi bobbidi boo all their worries away.

I've toured many shelters and other programs over the years and in most cases they either feel sterile or are complete chaos. Seldom have I walked into a place and it felt like home. I once asked a director at one of these surgical room shelters what caused the feeling. "It's by design," he told me.

"Why?" I inquired.

"Because if people feel like they are at home, they will never leave."

What an odd logic that was. Over my life I have lived in many different homes. I've moved out of rentals because I wanted to live in a different part of town or to move into a place that was cheaper. People move for a lot of different reasons and often it's for social ones like moving up the ladder or wanting to reshape their budget. The idea of creating an environment that is intentionally uninviting seems wholly against the purpose and mission of charity. Our goal shouldn't be to remind people of their lot in life or to make sure they "know their place" but rather to propel them into success and one of the greatest ways to do that is though praise, acknowledging milestones, and even a little bit of magic.

So at our little cold weather home we started having birthday parties. It seems like a small endeavor, but it produced some amazing results.

For these children, all they wanted was something that felt more than just home, they wanted that feeling of magic, that maybe this was the wardrobe into Narnia. One particular birthday will always stand out in my memory as the pinnacle of why this was such an important part of creating that environment of inclusion. There was a single mother who was staying with her daughters at the shelter and just a few days before they moved into their new home, the oldest daughter would be celebrating her birthday. More than anything she loved *Frozen* and so the volunteers got her an Elsa cake and purchased presents. Before dinner that night, she blew out her candles and celebrated as a happy child. She jumped for joy as she opened her presents and it was a truly happy day.

This wasn't some uniform event either; it wasn't like we kept sheet cakes in the freezer to pull out for the generic obligation of performing some idealistic ritual. One of the few rules we had for our volunteers at the shelter was that they couldn't give out gifts or money. There were a million reasons for this policy, one of which was we didn't want to create an environment of favoritism. But you are allowed to be the special center of attention on your birthday! These events were when the volunteers could really go all out. They would pick someone to do the birthday cake and then people would spend weeks trying to figure out what would be the perfect presents and they would all pool together the funding to make it happen. These parties were more about us being a big family. If you attended them, you couldn't tell who was who, guest, volunteer, staff… It was just a bunch of folks who cared about each other laughing and having a good time.

It changed the culture of the environment. The results spoke for themselves.

Later that week, we all gathered together again, this time to help them pack all their earthly belongings, including her new presents, into the back of a truck. Right before they left, the oldest daughter ran over and gave me a hug, saying, "This is the best hotel I've ever stayed at!

None of the others gave me a birthday party!" And with that they drove off to begin their new life in their new home.

So much of what we do working with people dealing with a crisis is focused on just that, the crisis. When we focus on the crisis, and not the person, then we inadvertently allow classism and separatism to seep in. We are the authors of the stories we tell. Every single day, when we walk into our office, board rooms or out into the field, we are the ones who make the decisions. We have the power to say yes or no, to wave the wand that will give someone lifesaving treatment, a new gown for prom or a place to call home ... at least for now. You are the fairy godmother. Finding unique and special ways to rejoice in the life of our clients, to focus on the positives, and to seek out opportunities to praise those we are serving are vital to creating success for them. Even if our goal is to be an emotional hospital, we don't have to make the environment feel like one.

No Record of Wrongs

How then do we move from this sterile feeling to creating an atmosphere of home? It is all about how we view our clients. Far too often we are guilty of looking at those we are called to help through a tainted lens. Instead of seeing their humanity, we are looking at them as just another churning wheel in the circle of need. Even the most difficult clients are most likely reacting out of their personal pain and fear. We have a responsibility to break down those anxieties and instead provide them a place where they feel genuinely safe. One of the easiest ways to do this is to rejoice with them, praise their successes and not only focus on the potential for failure. If we are honest with ourselves, all of the rules and regulations in place in most charities are based upon the presumption that our clients will fail or take advantage of generosity, not that they will succeed. The negative approach is embedded in our foundation, which is why it's time to rebuild.

I was eighteen years old when I first learned a valuable lesson about how to love in a genuine way. I was working hard but had personally found myself in a position where I didn't have enough money to make it to a funeral for a family member. I was talking about that experience with a friend of mine and lamented the fact that I was going to be unable to attend the funeral and how sad it made me feel.

"Why can't you go?"

"I just simply can afford it at the moment."

And with that my friend offered to loan me the cash to make the trip. They didn't just want to give me gas money, which was the part I was worried about, they took it a step further and offered to loan me enough money to make the drive, to get food, and to stay in a hotel. It was a very generous offer but I was reluctant to accept it. I wasn't certain when I would be able to pay them back and it was far more than I had ever asked for. But after I expressed all of my concerns they offered me some words of wisdom and it has been something I've carried with me every day since as my personal motto on the subject.

"If I give you this money, I'm not doing it as a loan; I am doing it because I love you. If you are ever able to pay me back one day, I'll be grateful. But if you aren't able to, I'll never mention this again."

And that was true, it was many years before I was in a place where I felt like I was able to pay this person back, but I had finally reached a small measure of success. Even though they claimed that the gift would never be on their mind, it was something I had always thought about. I was eager to be able to return their kindness. When I called them on the phone to ask for their address in order to be able to send them the funds, my friend laughed.

"Well, if you say I gave you the money, I'll be happy to take it back. But I don't even remember."

I believe they were being honest. They had made this belief system so part of their world view that they genuinely didn't ever think of it again. It's as if the debt had been permanently erased from their brain. It was in that moment I realized what it means to keep no record of wrongs. I'm sure that there are others who had not paid my friend back but if that were true, it wasn't being used against me in that moment. This also created a feeling of family and we've always shared a kinship as a result of the mutual love and respect we've shared over the years.

And this is the very way in which we create that same feeling of "home" for those who are displaced into our care. It isn't about holding them accountable to the sins of others and our charity certainly shouldn't be about seeing a return. It is about doing the right thing for the sake of it being the right thing. Charity is love; charity is about creating a sense of family. Upmost, it should be about bringing Heaven to Earth, a place where we have already prepared the banquet and there are rooms for everyone in the Divine Parent's mansion. Is it any wonder that our homeless king, who could find no room at the inn, decided to prepare a place for us where there would always be enough room?

So how are we making people feel at home? I mean this in the broader sense of the word. Are we creating waiting areas that make people feel valued instead of like they are on the chopping block? Whenever I walk into somewhere and the chairs are falling apart and the paint on the walls makes me feel like I'm in a prison, I shudder. There are always volunteers willing to step up and help in a million different ways. Put together a team that makes beautification a priority. If you change the way you show value to your clients and you change the way you interact with them, you'll see both a change in response and an increase in success.

Build into the framework of your organization a system of praising folks. Make the extra investment to give out gift cards for milestones and awards for achievements. But don't make it uniform, design it to be personal. Write real letters to your clients, letting them know what you are seeing in them and that you know they are trying hard. When you start to treat folks like they are loved and valued, there will be an absolute cultural shift.

Does that mean there won't be moments when you'll have to bring down the hammer? Of course there will be. I also can guarantee you that you'll be taken more seriously when those moments come if you typically lead with praise. If all our clients receive is despair that meets their own, it perpetuates the cycle. When we take the time to praise and rejoice along with them, in those rare moments when we do have to bring a chastisement, it stands out and it will also be listened to because a relationship has been built of mutual joy and trust.

Cheers!

As a young child going to church at least twice a week, there were certain catchphrase Christian terms that I would hear often, and over time, sadly, lost their saltiness. One of those for me is the biblical adage that, "God loves a cheerful giver." It was a phrase used with frequency and it lost its potency. Whenever I hear the use of it today, I can still smell the casseroles and cling wrap ruminating from the fellowship hall. But if God really does love a cheerful giver, why are we so damned gloomy about it as a society? I think the reason comes down to the fact that we are no longer giving without expectation, we are giving with attachments. There are absolutely strings attached to our way of doing charity and we are trying to run those strings through the arms and legs of the receivers in order to make them into puppets.

I know that this accusation may come with a bit of a sting and the truth is it's not your fault! We are still practicing as a society our great grandfathers' charity and not something based upon recent evidence or proven best practices. We are forcing people into a mold that they are unable to fit into and then becoming frustrated with their inability to live up to our outdated expectations. We aren't rejoicing with folks in their victories, we are demanding conformity. We've stopped trying to use our generosity to empower others and instead we are allowing it to be a weapon to try to clone others into emulating us. Even if we have a good model, that doesn't mean the model has to feel like a mold or a cookie cutter. It should feel like a friend taking us by the hand and leading us along the way.

At all of our volunteer orientations, we always have a question and answer time. Sure, we cover all the basics, but there are concerns that are unique to each volunteer. One day, a young man asked me, "What do we do if someone shows up to the shelter and they are drunk? Should we call the police? Do we call you?"

"What do you do when one of your friends is drunk and might be a little unruly? Would you call the police on your friend just for being drunk?" I asked in response.

"Well, no… I wouldn't call the police on my friend. Not unless he was doing something violent or whatever. I guess I would make them some coffee, try to get them something to eat and get them to bed."

"That sounds very reasonable. I think that's what you should do for your friends at the shelter too."

We don't encourage people to drink; as a matter of fact, we discourage it, even if that isn't their particular vice. We do so to encourage an environment where those who are struggling with alcoholism aren't tempted. From time to time, people will fall off the wagon. Just as we praise them when they are doing well, we try not to demean them when they fall. We reach down and help lift them up when they can't stand because that's what you do for people you love because, eventually, they will be able to stand on their own.

Just because we are practicing charity doesn't mean we have to look at those whom we are serving as charity cases. When we "other" those who we want to help we do both them and ourselves a great disservice. This is why it has always been the practice of any organization I have worked for in any capacity to require the volunteers to eat with the clients. Whenever it is possible, we don't even serve the food but rather use the "grandma's table" method and everyone makes their own plates, their own portion sizes, and picks their own chair to sit in. When the volunteers and staff actually take the time to sit down and listen to the clients' stories around the common ground of the dinner table, it breaks down a social barrier. It's no longer an us/them but an "all of us together" working toward the common good of helping these individuals graduate out of homelessness and into whatever success will look like for them. It's about honoring and glorifying them as individuals, not just in their actions but also in their desires and tastes.

Individualism is the singular most important part of this. Just as different people want different things on their plate, different people gauge success using a personalized metric, and what will be considered a successful graduation will be as unique as the person. For some of the families we served, that was as dramatic as them moving out of the shelter and into the first home they would purchase. However, for some of the single women who stayed with us, their success was a few of them all moving into a mobile home as roommates. For others, it was moving back in with family after making a recovery. But we rejoiced in all of these situations.

Each non-profit is different. How you will praise and rejoice along with your clients will be as unique as you and they are. I'm not attempting to create a system here; I'm talking about an ideological shift. This same principle is used within for profit businesses. When you make your customers feel valued, welcomed, and a part of the environment, then they feel a sense of ownership. They want to see the place's success. They go out of their way to invite their friends to have a coffee there or will praise the place on social media. Rejoicing is contagious and when we praise others, they praise us right back. It's about creating a culture of thanks and value.

For us, sometimes we would hold parties, other times one of the volunteers who worked really hard on a particular case would take them out to dinner. Other times we would help provide the client with all new furniture for their home. It was truly dependent on each situation because we had taken the time to sit down and listen to these folks. They had become our friends because we were willing to break the fourth wall and just let our hearts love. And because we had been in the mud with them, since we had battled alongside them and truly understood the struggle, it meant we knew how to actually rejoice with them in a personal way once the time came. And, for us, that made all the difference.

CHAPTER EIGHT

Bears All Things

Charity separates the rich from the poor; aid raises the needy and sets him on the same level with the rich.
Eva Peron

How We Got Here

It is sometimes difficult to look back over the map of someone's life and find the ground zero of what actually lead to their homelessness. In many cases, it becomes equivalent to the question of which came first, the chicken or the egg. When it comes to the failures of the system that is supposed to help them rise out from their plight, it is a bit easier to detect. Unfortunately, detection is not the same thing as solution. It is also more difficult to sell. No one wants to hear they've been doing something wrong, right? Lots of people have died on hills fighting for injustice or bad schools of thought, both physically and metaphorically. We have to collectively make a decision to be willing to make changes as necessary, not just to one portion of the non-profit sector but to the entire system.

There are few things in life as difficult as admitting when we are wrong and it's no less difficult for an organization that has been operating in good faith to admit that their methods don't line up with the best practices that produce results. But the truth is you can't feed or blanket someone out of homelessness, you can't paperwork someone's cancer away, and well wishes won't build an orphanage. For those of us who work in the area of homelessness specifically, one of the difficult realities to face is that not everyone will leave their addictions behind. So we are faced with an important and fundamental question, "Is our goal substance abuse recovery or ending homelessness?" Those are two very different things and it's only been prejudice and ideology that has allowed these two very unique issues to become intertwined.

The rehousing success rate for most non-profits that are tasked with helping the homeless is embarrassingly low. If you were to ask any of the well-intentioned volunteers or employees at the organizations, they would likely tell you that the reasons these low numbers exist are because the clients refuse to follow the programming regulations, because these individuals refuse to take the steps necessary to recover from substance abuse, and therefore the rehousing failure rests upon the client and not on the conscience of the organization itself. But substance abuse is not limited to those who live on the streets. There are alcoholics in the suburbs and there are billionaires addicted to drugs, so we can clearly see that substance abuse, in and of itself, is not the root cause of homelessness. You can have these problems in your life and still be rich; you can have them in your life and still be poor. The difference between a wealthy drug addict and one living on the streets is the well-to-do addict can buy better drugs. We have to come to terms with the unspoken truth that the actual cause of homelessness is not drugs, alcohol, laziness or any other excuse. The cause of homelessness is not having a home. The cure then is equally as simple, having a home.

Remarkably, very few organizations tasked with addressing poverty and homelessness have "ending homelessness" as their main mission statement. Rather, they are substance abuse programs with a focus on helping those experiencing homelessness address the symptoms of their addiction and not the cause of being without a house. If your main goal is not ending homelessness, you are simply an outreach program to people on the streets. Not that there is a problem with outreach. Obviously, everyone needs to eat, everyone needs to have a warm blanket in the cold, and these first-aid responses must continue in the interim period until someone is housed. But these things, in and of themselves, will never end homelessness as a whole. Sure, you can find some stories of success in low numbers. Where you see those numbers skyrocket is when we start focusing on ending the actual problem and digging deep into the pit of our society that has allowed homelessness to exist at all. However, until we are willing to do the hard work of staring down the social reform that must come to change how we view the problem and the cure, we will always simply be putting a Band-Aid on a bullet wound.

Again, this is me speaking out of my particular market experience. But this is actually a universal problem across the entire sector. We've seen numerous organizations shift focus from, "How do we find kids quickly when they are kidnapped?" to "How do we reduce kidnappings?" And the list is truly endless. Now, I feel as if it goes without saying that we would never say, "We should totally stop trying to find kids who are kidnapped." That is not the approach. Of course we should still do this! In that same way, it's why I don't discourage people from handing out food or blankets in their communities. We must help people survive in the interim, but we have to also become hyper focused on the long-term solution. This is true for every single organization, we need to attend to the surrounding problems and be attentive to the long-term cure.

Here is where things become dangerous. There are so many organizations built around the exterior issues that they start to become dependent on the cure never being found. That's a controversial truth to say but it must be said repeatedly. We should not be building empires out of need, we should be building pop-up stores addressing the crisis, resolving the problem, and quickly moving on to the next issue.

In my field, the source of the problem was birthed out of a recovery model that became the norm within the non-profit sector that focuses on addressing homelessness known as: Housing Ready. This ideology was fostered out of a mistaken worldview that essentially said, "The homeless are experiencing this state because of an action they have done: drugs, alcohol or laziness. In order for them to recover, they simply have to become sober or be endowed with a work ethic. Then, and only then, will they be able to pull themselves up by their boot straps and be well." There exists one major flaw with this ideology: It's not based in reality.

The more we have begun to learn about the root causes of homelessness the more we've come to realize that the vast majority of those experiencing any state of being un-housed are in this position due to circumstances outside of their control and not substance abuse. Many of those who are currently living on the streets that do have a substance abuse problem did not pick up the habit before they fell into hard times but, rather, afterward as a way of coping with their situation. It's a form of self-medication. And for those few who did find themselves homeless because of their substance abuse, they will find it nearly impossible to seek the recovery they need while they are in survival mode. As a matter of fact, most ethical recovery programs will not even admit someone unless they have stable housing. How is someone supposed to be living in fear and misery, which is the cause of addiction, and also recover from the substance that is helping them escape that feeling? The mental hooks of addiction are, in most cases, because we are attempting to escape pain in our lives. In order to recover from substance abuse, a person needs to feel safe, secure, and loved. An unstable living situation is almost a surefire way to guarantee failure for a client attempting to recover.

The ideology that motivates the Housing Ready model is essentially that, in order to graduate to housing, a person must be able (or ready) to independently take on housing. They need to be recovered from any and all vices in order to transition into housing. If they are unwilling or unable to do so, continuing to live on the streets is the natural consequence of this decision. How ironic is it that the vast majority of homeless outreach programs are operated by religious organizations, groups that from the pulpit would preach that we are saved by grace and not by works, and will in turn require a works-based model in order to be saved from the streets? A home in Heaven requires nothing except faith, but in order to receive a temporal home here on Earth, *that* requires you to earn your keep. In reality, this is not only a model that has proven to be factually ineffective; it's not even theologically sound.

If we are going to live out our charity in a way that is in unison with the heart of a loving God, then it should follow in the footsteps of grace. Grace meets us in the streets, waiting at the road with a robe and ring, ready to prepare a feast. It bears the burden with us; it takes the yoke around its neck to help carry the load. It doesn't cast judgment but rejoices in the good, weeps with us, and leads us on the road step by step.

Homeward Bound

Everything has a first, and my first exposure to housing initiatives working positively was when I traveled to Texas to witness a program I had been hearing positive things about. They had a low bar of entry and it was working, it was a model I had hoped to duplicate. So we decided to test it out for ourselves. "What would happen if we pulled out all of the stops?" The goal of this project was to gauge theories of a successful model against the reality of their implementation in our own community. We essentially threw out every rule that had ever been written and started at zero. We required no identification, no drug testing, no "proof of homelessness" or any of the other policies that have infiltrated themselves in the consciousness of the charity mindset. Guess what? It wasn't easy; it was actually pretty damn difficult. And we ran into many problems. But they were our problems, unique problems, and we were finding modern solutions to address them.

Because we had no rules, we didn't have a basis for rejecting anyone. That was the point but it also became the issue. We were supposed to be a shelter specifically for families and single women. However, what defines a family? Children? I suppose that was my personal philosophy when we opened the doors, but that was challenged immediately when a middle-aged woman and her husband came knocking on our door seeking help for their family. Well, I suppose that is a family. Of course it's a family! Not everyone wants or is able to have children but that doesn't change the fact that they loved each other and cared for each other, and, most importantly in this situation, were homeless together. A family experiencing homelessness, that's what we were there to respond to … right?

According to them, they both lost their jobs within weeks of each other and suddenly everything fell apart. This is a common narrative and, when you think about it logically, it makes absolute sense. For folks working in jobs where they can be terminated without cause, that includes missing work because of illness, as was the case with this couple. She got sick and took a few days off from work; he took a few days off to attend to her needs. They were both terminated for missing work and being human.

This is one of those areas where it is so important for all of us in the non-profit world to work together to create systems in unison. These folks needed help outside of our area of expertise; there were potential legal recourses available to them. They needed assistance from local job finder resources. Connectivity of services is key to survival. Not only does it reduce duplication of services but it streamlines the process for the client. Can you imagine if instead of every organization trying to reinvent the wheel, we just worked together with other agencies who were already doing it well? That's why it's important to ask ourselves, "Is this already happening in my community?" Instead of attempting to do what is already being done, working alongside folks who are doing it well is far more beneficial to those you want to help.

So here I was being faced with an unmet need. I had taken in this family of husband and wife but then suddenly I was feeling a high level of guilt as the rooms began to fill up. Of course these folks were a family, but soon I would have to reject a family with children over a family without children. What was I supposed to do?

Well, the most logical thing to do if you have someone who is without a home and you need them out of the shelter, well, just place them in a house because then a magical thing happens—they aren't homeless anymore. And a few days later, the perfect opportunity came my way.

A friend of mine who owned a mobile home complex happened to have a unit come available and lost their maintenance person recently. They contacted me to see if anyone was looking for work at our shelter and offered a mobile home in exchange for helping out around the complex. But there was one catch; the home was way too small for a family with children. I knew just the people to approach. Within just a few days of them accessing services at our shelter, they were in a home and employed. They instantly began to thrive and became an essential asset to my friend's company. As of the time of this writing, they are still employed at the company and are still housed after all these years. That is qualifiable success because they were housed *first*. Would they have failed a drug test? Are they functional alcoholics? I don't know because we didn't ask those questions. We didn't engage them under the presumption of guilt. We took them in just as they were and provided them with the first opportunity we could to engage them in housing. And it worked. They would be just the first of many.

How We Recover

When we bear the burden with our clients, it makes all of the difference in the world. The ugly truth about how we have been functioning as a non-profit culture is that we have spent too much time focusing on the symptoms and not the cure. We've been placing Band-Aids on bullet wounds. If the culture does not shift away from symptoms and rather towards the cure, we will never see the type of change that must take place to resolve whatever issue we are trying to resolve. The problems we face as a community of caregivers are unique but the fix is universal. We have to take up the mantle with our clients.

One of the fundamental questions we have to ask ourselves is, "Does our organization put forward a mission of ending the problem or just addressing the problems surrounding the issue?" This is a difficult but finite difference in how we operate and it affects how we quantify success. If our goal is simply to distribute goods to those in need, we only gauge success based upon what we put out and not results. We praise our success based solely upon what we've given away and not by how many people we have truly relieved of the core problem we are designed to address. This is not to say that we don't need these social justice programs that provide a resource, we certainly do. We need to make sure that people aren't going to bed hungry or without daily necessities. However, toothbrushes and tube socks aren't going to end someone's homelessness any more than a hot meal will. These are just symptoms of the greater problem, a problem that exists in all segments of our charity programs.

If these social outreaches are not directly tied to providing people with evacuation services, then they are simply part of the circular nature of need. As the scripture puts it, "Suppose a brother or sister is without clothes or daily food. If one of you says to them, 'Go in peace; keep warm and well fed,' but does nothing about their physical needs, what good is it?" In this same way, we've stopped short of fixing the problem by addressing the surface level needs. We've made sure, in many ways, that we've met people's day-to-day necessities, but we're not attaching these temporary solutions to long-term ones in order to bring people out of the need. We treat everything like a hospice, when in fact most people just need an ER visit.

This approach is impractical and lacking in genuine compassion, but it's also expensive. When we take the time to calculate the cost of providing someone all of the services they interact with throughout the course of the year, from meals, emergency services and hospitals to even jailing folks for basic human functions like sleeping, we are spending countless thousands of dollars on each person we engage with each year as a community. We also have little to show for it. Some reports have claimed the national rehousing success rate of "housing ready" models to be roughly 8%. We should all take a pause at what dismal a report card that truly is. However, with a long-term retention rate of 98%, rapid rehousing and the housing first model has proven itself to be the model showing genuine success.

In order to achieve this success, we have to change the way in which we are approaching the problem. We must remove the impediments that are preventing people from accessing services in the first place. This begins with no longer assuming guilt on our clients. Each case has to be evaluated on its own merits and not based upon regulations created to curb the potential of "abuse of the system". No level of abuse of an agency will ever cost more than it's currently costing per person to allow them to remain on the streets.

One of my favorite charities in my community provides meals to people who are living with AIDS. The whole model is built upon sustainability and resource access. The organization operates a catering company and the funds raised through their business model in turn supplement the cost of their outreach. But do you know what this organization also does? It partners with other groups that are helping find a cure for AIDS and also ones that help reduce infection rates. One day, when we really do have a cure, this agency will no longer be necessary—at least not in the way it exists now—and that's totally alright with them. The goal is to meet a real need in real time, but they aren't building an industry around that need. Instead, they have built a temporary business to address the need until the need no longer exists. They have borne the burden with their clients and met the need, while also addressing the broader issues of making sure there will be a day when the need is eliminated.

For this to truly work, we must bear the yoke with our brothers and sisters and lift the burden on our own shoulders as well, carrying it along with them. This should always be a team effort. We must be willing to adapt and admit the failures that have crept into our organizations, to make a cultural mea culpa. We must remove the notion that a person needs to reach a certain level of perfection in order to be worthy of our help and instead approach everyone with grace, accepting the same level of compassion that true love calls us to and echoing the message of grace and good news: Come just as you are.

CHAPTER NINE

Believes

All the Friars should preach by their deeds.
Saint Francis of Assisi

Clap Your Hands

The word "believe" has such a powerful meaning. It's far deeper than we give it credit for. The dictionary describes the word as, "accepting (something) as true." That idea has power and with that comes great responsibility. Sometimes we believe certain things to be true that have absolutely no merit whatsoever. These beliefs can be cultural, societal or just due to bad information. Once something becomes a belief, it can be difficult to change someone's mind on the subject. We can build whole systems around bad beliefs and misinformation; we fight wars over them, imprison people because of them, and deprive others of their rights ... all because we have a belief. People are even willing to die for their beliefs. During my years of pastoral ministry, I often reminded my congregants that they needed to be very careful about the things they came to "believe" because not every idea is worth dying on the mountain for. For a very long time, people genuinely believed the world was flat and refused to embark on certain levels of adventure and exploration because they believed the world would genuinely end with them falling off into an abyss. There were people who suffered severe consequences for believing against this idea, and yet the truth of reality prevailed in the end. People were willing to die, and others willing to kill, over something that would later be proven as a matter of science.

The power of our beliefs can change our world view and can even affect how we view others. More importantly, once a belief becomes so entrenched within our broader culture, it can shape the way that others see themselves. This is why it is so important that we dramatically change the narrative of how we communicate our clients' needs. In a very significant way, this responsibility rests on the shoulders of those of us who are tasked with serving them.

A few years ago, I was invited to speak at a forum on homelessness at a church. I listened as people asked a series of questions and so many of them were laced with prejudice. In some ways, I don't place the blame on those who were asking the questions. These ideologies have become so infiltrated in our culture that folks have come to believe that the narratives must be true to some extent. Tell a lie enough times and it becomes a truth.

Then a woman sitting in the back stood up and was handed the microphone. She cleared her throat and gently asked, "How deep do you think the stigma of homelessness goes?"

This is a profoundly important question and I commended her for asking it. What I explained that day was essentially this: We once had a woman staying at our shelter. For many years she told us she was able to avoid living on the streets because she was a sex worker. Though she was experiencing a type of homelessness, because she lived in a motel she was able to maintain a roof over her head. She had many small children and they would be sent out of the room to play on the sidewalk as men would come in and out of the room throughout the day. "I may have been a hooker but at least I wasn't homeless," she said to me. Even though she was now staying in a homeless shelter, she refused to accept the reality of her situation. She did not want to be labeled with that title.

This reality has stuck with me, that for her and many others, the stigma of homelessness is so great that this mother would rather be known as a street walker than a street dweller. Now, I would like to note the extreme love and devotion that this mother had for her children that she was willing to do literally anything for their survival.

There is no value in shaming men or women who work in the sex industry. This is something that those of us who work in the area of homelessness face every single day. However, I simply mention this anecdote to bring home the reality that, even though there exists a great amount of stigma associated with sex work, for this woman, admitting this reality was nothing near the stain of that damning word: homeless.

Our society has created a dangerous narrative and chooses to believe the worst about those experiencing homelessness. Lives quite literally hang in the balance and what we choose to allow others to believe about the plight of those experiencing homelessness has real-life consequences, not only in areas that are clearly defined and obvious, such as the examples I listed above, but also because this type of desperation leads to people making the ultimate escape through suicide. How often can you hear society define how you must be, in the vaguest and broadest assumptions possible, before it truly affects what you believe about yourself? When society believes you are a worthless bum, it leaves scars that can last long after the temporal circumstances of being unhoused are relieved.

This reality is true within every aspect of social justice work. For women and men who experience sex trafficking and feel they have no other value. For the woman who feels she can no longer be seen as sexual or beautiful after breast cancer. We must fight actively for the dignity, love, hope, and respect for our clients. This is why we all have to change entirely how we discuss their unique stories and experiences with the world. Anyone who works directly in the field of helping people who want to leave sex work will tell you that my narrative doesn't show the full spectrum. There are plenty of stigmas that go along with that reality too. So we must change the culture of how we communicate all of the narratives across the entire spectrum of the non-profit industry because what we say is a reflection of what we believe about a person, place or thing. This means that we have to adopt a complete change in how we communicate with those whom we are serving as well.

Bringing People First language into our area of service is paramount. Instead of utilizing language like, "the homeless person," we say, "a person experiencing homelessness." This is true across all fields; instead of, "the AIDS patient," try saying, "Michael is a person living with AIDS, he's also an amazing artist." This goes so much deeper into how we communicate with and about those whom we are caring for, referring to them not as, "the client," or by a case number but by name. People are not their circumstance. They are not a case file. They are individuals with real feelings, hopes, and dreams. In order to believe in them, and believe the best about them, we have to first see them as not just a project sitting on our desk to be filed. That change comes in how we communicate because our language has real power.

Positive Reinforcement

There are so many positive aspects of having and cherishing beliefs. It is in the realm of belief that we find hope, and that is one of the most powerful tools we have. In a world so devoid of feeling that real change is possible, belief and hope are essential. We simply must be careful in how we focus our beliefs and in what way we are displaying them.

If I were able to isolate one of the most controversial systems I have set in place at several of the organizations I've worked with, it has been removing any requirement of our clients to mandatorily participate in religious services. That was a hard sale. Most of our volunteers came from area churches or faith groups. Many shelters and service providers require people to go to church services, participate in prayer or other religious devotions in order to receive help from their agencies. But the question becomes is compulsory participation equal to genuine devotion? Or were these programs simply requiring people to perform song and dance routines for their meal? It's a tough question to ask and a lot of folks took initial offense to this.

A genuine belief isn't coerced or forced, it's accepted freely. If we take the time to believe in our clients and put our faith in them, they will feel that and those that wish to will respond to our good faith. Our actions should speak for themselves and we should not give in order to convert someone to our own ideologies by way of coercion. That is called colonialism.

If what we are providing has merit and meets a need, we should respond to and relieve the suffering regardless of whether someone conforms to our ideologies or not. Doing the right thing should be done for the sake of it being the right thing, and if the secondary effect is them accepting your world view, well then, I suppose that's icing on the cake. When we withhold help because someone doesn't see the world the same way we do, that isn't genuine love. There really isn't a precedent for that in the scriptures either. Jesus healed the centurion's servant, even though they didn't match ideologically. He also went on to heal a great many people and care for them in unique and special ways regardless of where their personal beliefs might lie. Why? Because He cared for the whole person. Though He expressed His personal truth, that didn't stop Him from caring for, and providing care to, people who didn't match with Him 100%. The scriptures say, "They will know you are my disciple by your love for one another." It is in our kindness, compassion, and love for one another that we live out the truth of our vocation, no matter which direction we kneel when we pray.

When we take the time to step back and believe in those we care about it, to put our faith in their future, we change the whole relationship. The nature of giving is supposed to be about letting go of the gift without expecting anything in return. When we attach a requirement to that, we must not really believe in what we are going to accomplish. It should go without saying that if your system works, it will work regardless of someone's personal belief structure. I think this is why programs based on the Twelve Steps have had decades of sustainable and quantifiable success. They have built within their structure that each person's own belief can fit within the broader spectrum of their individual healing. That system acknowledges a higher power but doesn't define what that might be for each person, whether that higher power is a finite understanding of a deity or just the belief in the great human will.

When we let go of mandating compliance to our practices, allowing our personal beliefs to be our individual motivation, but not a qualifying requirement for help, it changes the relationship from a power structure system to one of equality and partnership.

I Wanna Hold Your Hand

I have not agreed with every single client who has come to see me. And I'll say something most won't: There have been many that I've met that I don't generally like. Sure, I give them the same level of care, but there are just some personalities that don't really mesh and that's alright. There was someone I worked with who was ideologically in complete political opposition to me. He was quite the character. I would constantly encourage my volunteers not to engage in religious or political debates with clients, but this guy could always rope me in. I would be heading to a meeting or trying to complete some task and he would find a way to get my goat. Next thing I knew, we would be in some heated discussion about politics and locking horns. We would always find a way to call a truce and walk away on generally good terms. Whether I would have given that same grace to someone I wasn't working with is debatable in and of itself, but I digress.

One day, this client decided to get himself into one of these heated arguments with another resident. It did not go well at all and the end result was that they nearly engaged in a fist fight. This was the very reason why we discouraged these types of engagements at the shelter, but we aren't babysitters and we certainly can't monitor (nor should we) every single conversation that takes place.

The unfortunate reality of human nature is that disagreements can often lead to violence. That is the true danger of some beliefs.

So my debate buddy found himself in a pickle. He left the program huffing and puffing. He vowed never to return, but that didn't go very well for him because, as it turns out, he really did want to get his life back on track. He didn't want to continue to live outside, and he realized after he stepped away from the fight that he wanted to go back to receiving the care he was receiving. After a few days he called me. "I'm pretty embarrassed about what happened, but I can't come back. They aren't going to let me come back, even if you would."

I made an offer to him that I've made with countless others. "Brother, if I have to walk in there holding your hand and tell everyone that they've gotta come through me to get to you, I'll do it."

He returned later that day because he knew I had his back.

What he also knew was that I didn't agree with him. We did not see eye to eye and I didn't require him to pretend to be someone he wasn't in order to get help. My job wasn't converting him ideologically to my political or religious beliefs; my responsibility was to do whatever I could to help him get out of living on the streets and into permanent housing as quickly as possible. I was willing to stand beside him and protect him so that he could eventually have a home of his own where he would be able to express his own ideas and beliefs until he was blue in the face. Just as I have the luxury of doing. The purpose of helping should be to bring people to a goal and that goal should be personal actualization, not ideological alignment.

Within the non-profit world, we impose a lot of ideas on our clients and that can be dangerous. It's important to ask ourselves if we are imposing only what is necessary to see them succeed and not attaching other elements purely because we want to win other battles. Service should not be run by ideologues, even if our personal ideologies are what motivate us to do what we are doing. When our charity is truly actualized as an act of love, then it hopes for the best for a person but allows them the room to grow into whatever is best for them.

When we take the time to believe in our clients, we see different results. This goes back to that whole idea of treating each person as an individual. It's much more difficult to do, but the end results speak for themselves.

CHAPTER TEN

Hopes

*The simplest acts of kindness are by far more powerful
than a thousand heads bowing in prayer.*
Mahatma Gandhi

The Horizon

Hope is the belief in things yet to come. When I was a
child and my family went through our period of homelessness, hope was the only thing that kept me going. It
lay far out there like a guiding star, a thing to be obtained,
wished upon. I would believe for a future where things
would get better and I no longer had to see my mother
cry about unpaid bills or cops kicking us out of motel
rooms. I would watch hope well up in my father with each
new potential opportunity. But hope is something very
fragile and it can be dashed in an instant. Losing hope is
a very dangerous thing. The feeling that things cannot get
better or that there is no longer a future to hold on to,

that is where depression lies dormant, waiting to attack its prey. Apathy will take hold and we can become stuck in an endless cycle, wandering around in the desert with no horizon in sight.

I can remember very clearly the moments when hope would be instilled in me during those trying times, when certain people would rise to the occasion and hand hope over like precious stones for us to walk on until we reached the next phase of our lives. People would step up and make sure that, in the middle of all the chaos, my siblings and I could still celebrate Christmas. Other times, it was when a friend would let us stay at their home for a few nights. These moments, these simple acts of charity, became memories to cling to, to build upon and believe that maybe more benevolence was on the way, a lifeline to rescue us out of this circular pattern we had been stuck in for so long.

We often hear people of good intentions use the phrases, "They'll have to pull themselves up by their bootstraps," or that we need to give, "a hand up, not a hand out." But the problem is sometimes people don't have hands or can't afford boots. The shoes on their feet may have become so worn that they are waterlogged, the leather has dry rotted and when they pull on those straps, it gives way and they topple over. Others are born without hands or have lost them in an industrial steel mill accident.

Yes, we want to teach sustainability and personal responsibility when applicable; but when our system becomes so engrained with this mentality, we become rigid. We forget that not everyone has the same opportunities or ability. For these situations, hope lies in our ability to bend to meet the needs of the individual, not in our attempts to bend the individual to fit within our program. When we can learn to have this flexibility and write that into our programming, that is where hope meets grace. That is, at its purest form, genuine salvation. Justice.

As an adult, I can remember the first time I met someone who had lost all hope and it has haunted me for all of these years. It was the first year of my priesthood. As a young priest living in a world that was very much changing, there was a great deal of internal dialogue amongst the clergy about wearing clerical attire every single day. Many clergy had opted to forgo this tradition for many reasons. Maybe it was shame because of scandals within the church or they just wanted to enjoy their time in public without having to hear confessions at coffee shops. This attire was for us both a mark and distinction of our vocation, but it could also be a burden that came with a great many stigmas attached. One such night, I was walking downtown and speaking with a close friend of mine about this very topic and my mind was made up for me when a man in tattered clothing ran up to us. He stopped abruptly right in front of me and fell to the ground crying out in genuine despair.

"Father, please forgive me!" he cried with absolute abandon.

I knelt down next to the man and looked at him. He smelled of alcohol and urine. The hem of his pants had ripped down the center, leaving his genitals exposed. He had reached a point of such depression that he no longer cared. He was, quite literally, naked before the entire world—emotionally and physically. Something we are all taught about in church and are supposed to be hyper aware of is that shame of our own nakedness is the curse of the fall of man. But, to me, this man had fallen as far as a man could fall and here he lay, naked before the whole world without any shame. Tears rolled down his dirt-stained cheeks, making deep caverns of grief on his weathered face. He looked up at me and his empty eyes broke through and looked directly into my soul.

"Forgive me, Father, forgive me, please! Forgive my sins so I can kill myself and be with my son."

"What is it you need forgiveness for?" I asked in the most solemn voice I could muster, emulating what I must have imaged at the time I was supposed to sound like. None of my pastoral training had prepared me for a moment such as this. Finally, he explained his original request with more detail.

"My son, he died. He was killed at sea. He was my only son and I cannot live with myself anymore. I was supposed to protect him. I am his daddy and my one job was to protect him. I couldn't do it and I can't live with this anymore. Tonight, I was heading to the water to kill myself. I got drunk and was going to the water to throw myself in to drown and finally be with my son again. I know what I am going to do is a sin. Can you forgive me before I take my life? I can't go on anymore. But I want to be in Heaven with my son."

The determination in his voice was certain. In his mind he was already dead and he was simply about to help his body catch up with his reality. He grabbed my hands and placed them on his face as he wept into them. I was rushed with a sense of responsibility. How I acted in this moment, the things that I said and did, would have real-life consequences. If I betrayed this man's trust or hurt him in any way, he would continue on his deadly path. He was not asking for me to stop him, he was asking for me to assure him and give him absolution to continue on his journey of destruction. He was without home or redemption in his own heart. He had, without question, given up any sense of purpose, there was nothing waiting for him in the future. So it became my responsibility, in this moment, to be for him what he no longer had within himself: hope.

I lay there on the street with him and I listened to his story. We spoke for hours about his son and about his life and the things that led him to this moment. I recounted with him my own experiences, the moments when I felt that I had reached such a deep sense of loss that I, too, wondered if the world would in fact be a better place if I wasn't here. We drank water together; I held him as he cried. Neither of us paid any mind to those who walked by in bewilderment at the scene playing out before them. I gave up my own sense of pride and instead I did what we are called to do as priests, I stood in His place. I prayed with him and I promised him that I would not let this be the end. And as the moments moved on, he slowly began to sober up. The realization of what he had almost done began to break through as logic and reason welled up, no longer pushed down by intoxication.

"Can you help me?"

"Yes, I can."

We stood up together and I drove him to the hospital and he went through the intake process to be admitted under the Baker Act. He wanted to get sober, for good this time. He wanted to build a life worth living again. And, more importantly, he wanted to be instilled again with a sense of purpose and hope. He wanted to live.

I had hope, too, enough to spare. I believed that the system was designed to catch him. That I would drive him to the hospital, that he would be admitted and care would be given. That there would be a shelter to take him in and provide him with what was needed in order to restore his life back to what it had originally been. We drove together, me with my hope and him with his borrowed hope. There were many realities we faced that evening and over the coming days, ones that would leave both of us disappointed as hope was forced into the square peg of reality.

A Lost Cause

It goes without saying that a great many of those whom we are called to serve have reached a point during this experience with poverty and homelessness of giving up hope. Almost everyone I have spoken with over the years has expressed that they have wanted to take their own lives because of the extreme depression they have felt living on the streets. They have gone down deep into the depths of feeling truly worthless. One man once said to me, "It's not that I think the world would be better without me. It's that I'm so insignificant it just doesn't even matter if I am here." That is without question the purest definition of losing hope. But what happens when not only those who are experiencing homelessness lose hope but also those of us who are supposed to be providing them a pathway out lose hope in them?

During a pretty tumultuous time for our community regarding homeless issues, one of the service providers invited an expert on the subject to come do a series of community meetings to discuss ways that we could re-develop our thinking on poverty. Over the weekend, he spoke at numerous churches and non-profits and each session was to deal with a different aspect of the issues surrounding poverty. I attended all the meetings and there was something that I couldn't help but notice that was lacking from his lectures. He had spoken on community redevelopment, ways in which charities were failing the community and also pathways for them to help clients avoid homelessness. However, he didn't really touch on the issue of how to help people get back out of home-lessness, just how to avoid it. In his mind, it was better never to let the clients reach the streets in the first place. Now, I of course agreed with this ideology on the surface. It is certainly better that no one ever experiences home-lessness and, from a general cost analysis, it is absolutely cheaper to catch someone before they fall than it is to rebuild their life from the proverbial "rock bottom".

So, during his last lecture, during the question and answer time, I posed my query. "What do you think is the best way to help build up resources for those who are currently living on the streets? Shelters? An aggressive housing first model? What is the answer?"

He paused for a moment before answering. "Well, those folks have succumbed to drugs and alcohol, those people living on the streets. I suppose the shelters are the best place for them."

"What resources should we be working toward to make the shelters better so they have a higher rehousing rate?"

"I would think that, for most of them, they aren't going to want to get the help they need."

And, with that, many of the hundreds of people in the audience, most of whom were service providers or volunteers, nodded their heads in agreement. It seemed that our "expert" had given up hope in those who are often called "the least of these." Worse, he had a chorus of nodding heads agreeing with his assertion.

The dangerous reality is that many non-profit organizations have played hot potato with the issue of the most difficult clients: The Rock Bottomers. For decades, the rehousing success rates have been so low that some justification has had to be made to explain away this phenomenon. Instead of us shouldering the blame and admitting that somewhere along the way we have failed those whom we are called to serve, we have passed on that blame down to those on the streets, handing it off to the clients themselves. Perpetuating the idea that they want to live this way or that they are somehow the authors of their own destruction. Forgetting that the vast majority of them ended up homeless because of issues outside of their control—

mental illness, physical disabilities, they are the victims of abuse, being rejected by their families because of their sexual orientation or gender identity or they are returning war veterans with limited resources. They are folks who lost their homes because of the market crash, oil spills, and a never-ending cycle of economic uncertainty mixed with a unbalanced power structure. They are folks that have lost all hope because the world decided that it didn't have a place for them. They somehow slipped through the wide gaps of our social safety nets. Gaps that we all know exist but once we watch someone fall through them, we look down the hole as they fall and say, "What did you do wrong?" knowing full well in our own hearts, if we are honest with ourselves, that what went wrong is that our structure is not set up for success. And if we followed models exemplified in other industries, we would have higher success rates.

We've lost sight of our purpose, no longer focusing on the call that is universal to all who carry forward the mission of charity: It is our responsibility to be hope where hope no longer exists.

Standing in the Gap

What does it truly mean to be a giver of hope? I think in its purest form it means that it's our responsibility not only to provide a service—food, medical treatment, shelter for families waiting on a loved one to be released from the hospital or shelter in general—but to walk hand in hand with them along the journey, believing genuinely for a brighter future. We have to stop looking at our clients as stuck within a particular station in life and actually believe that there is still potential and value in each and every person that we meet. If we do not, what is the purpose of our doing what we do each and every single day? Why do we stay up late hours filling out grant paperwork and working on major holidays, missing time with our own families? Is it just for the sake of doing it? Is it just because it is the right thing to do? I can't imagine that is truly enough for most of us who do this work day in and day out.

It is certainly easy to give up hope. We see at close range people fall each and every single day. Many times we see people we truly thought were on a road to recovery jump right off the wagon. We watch with crushing blows as someone we had put so much faith in loses yet another job and it weighs on our souls. We take these stories home with us and they rattle around in our brains as we try to enjoy dinner with our families. We see people we love and care for rummage through trash behind restaurants we are leaving. Those of us who have devoted our lives to this work live in an odd space between normalcy and the third world of America that everyone pretends doesn't exist.

Without question, the temptation then is to become frustrated with our clients, our friends. How could they do this? Why were they late to work again? How is it possible they missed their meeting with the social security attorney? I worked hard to get them that chemotherapy appointment and they didn't show up, don't know they know this is life and death? But if we take a step back and are honest with ourselves, have we given them all the tools they need to truly succeed? So much of the non-profit industrial complex that we have built is reliant on opposed systems working in conjunction with each other in ways that are nearly impossible. We know that the odds are stacked against our clients for success. Sure, we fight for someone to get their social security, but we also know, deep down, that no one can live off of $800 dollars a month. We are missing whole pieces of the puzzle. Yet, the system we work from prohibits us from certain levels of political engagement to speak out on the very issues that we see harming our clients.

In other words, we have lost hope that these people we serve can actually get back on their feet. Sure, we all have those amazing success stories that we put on the back of brochures or share on social media in hopes that it will go viral and raise awareness about the causes that are important to us. But we allow the narrative of failure to drive our day-to-day practices. With this, we have now created a dangerous world where the idea of failure is captaining the ship. But what if the failure isn't the client? What if it's actually us? The system itself was never designed for success. It was designed reactively to an influx of poverty, homelessness, sickness, and violence. We began to just throw food and blankets at the problem and then walk around baffled as to why people can't drive a bowl of soup to a job interview or why a blanket doesn't cuddle someone out of schizophrenia.

We haven't just lost hope in the clients. We've lost hope in ourselves and in the whole system that we are a part of. It is past time that we move on beyond this infectious feeling of hopelessness and instead become a lighthouse again, a resting place. We must make genuine and fundamental changes to every aspect of how we operate. We must reform the old ways of doing things and, sometimes, as painful as it may be, we have to abandon the familiar. We have been putting new wine into old wineskins and walking around confused about why they burst. Our system is broken, but there is, without question, a pathway forward for change.

However, in order to truly be able to accomplish this goal we have to begin again with a sense of hope, a belief not only in our clients but also within ourselves. There is a reason why we are failing at the success we want to achieve. We are no longer looking with belief toward the future. We have stagnated in the present. The non-profit sector has ceased to be innovators. Of course, we see glimpses of it, videos that are shared a million times online, and we think, *Wow! That's amazing … but it wouldn't work within my own non-profit.*

A perfect example of innovation within the non-profit sector is the Empowerment Plan. A young college student, Veronica Scott, saw a need within her community in Detroit. People were cold and living on the streets. She invented a coat that could be turned into a sleeping bag. That could have been the end of it, but she didn't stop there. The demand for the coat grew and people all over the country wanted to buy them to give out in their own communities. This is where she stepped away from what most non-profits would do and walked into a territory only seen in the businesses sector. When faced with this type of supply and demand, we would scramble to find volunteers and offer the product at an extremely undervalued rate. She did not do this. Instead, she opted to provide a quality product at a fair price and turned around and hired those whom she had previously been helping, creating a system of sustainability. It was bold; it was dangerous; it was entrepreneurship within a non-profit context.

If we are going to create real change within our industry (and let's make no mistake about it, it is an industry), then we will have to make fundamental and bold changes.

Then we have to identify the link between the spirit of entrepreneurship and the non-profit sector—hope. We hope for a future yet to come, a place yet unseen, and worlds yet to be discovered. It's that boldness that harnessed electricity, believed we could fly, and finally got us to the moon. In the last decade we've seen dramatic changes in how we communicate and socialize; media has brought us to the forefront of a new frontier, a second Wild West. But as we've watched all these changes happen before our eyes, we've still got non-profits using fax machines. There are apps to be invented that could streamline services and cut our time doing paperwork in half and project our clients' success to industry-leading standards. We just have to be willing to take the bold risks and step out of our comfort zone and be willing to look weird. And just so you know, we already do … we just aren't reaping the same rewards as Silicon Valley, not because we couldn't but because we aren't taking the steps necessary to get us there.

We have to be willing to listen, innovate, and to stand in the gap. We must be hope for the hopeless.

CHAPTER ELEVEN

Endures

> *It is the apathetic person that sees the cause while the charitable person sees the need.*
> *Shannon L. Alder*

The Rat Race

The scriptures tell us, "Let us run with endurance the race God has set before us." And what a great race it is for those of us who are called to serve the ones who have become society's "new lepers". Throughout all time, cultures have created people who are outcast and abandoned. It seems that no sooner is liberation on the horizon for one marginalized group than our society picks a new target of oppression. The end game for most people who are ostracized within our culture, more often than not, is that they experience abandonment and then homelessness. This is where the importance of intersectionality of cause and cure comes into play. Within the charity world, which is vast and touches on everything from a cure for cancer to transportation solutions to providing food for the elderly, we are all doing it because we engage with clients who cannot afford, for one reason or another, something that others are privileged to have access to easily.

Even though what poverty and homelessness has looked like throughout the ages has certainly changed with the times, it has always had the same cure: a home.

When we look at how God is presented in the Christian scriptures and what our Creator desires for us as a people, it has always been a sense of belonging, a place to call home, starting with Eden, then the Promised Land, and ultimately the New Jerusalem in that mystical place we call Heaven. Christ even said that as he was leaving us he would go to, "…prepare a place for you. A house with many rooms." That longing to have a place to call our own, to be part of a family and to be secure, is something that all human beings long for. It is part of our personhood and psychology, belonging to a culture group is imbedded into our emotional DNA. Maslov's hierarchy of needs places having somewhere to call our own as a basic human need. Food, water, and shelter are at the base of the pyramid of needs that each and every person has at the very core of their being. So within the psychological understanding of needs, we learn that if we do not have these base needs met, we cannot achieve personal fulfillment of our goals.

This philosophy also teaches us that without these basic human needs being met something very dangerous happens, we transition into survival mode. We are no longer operating with logic and reason but using our base animal instincts to simply stay alive. It is the reason why people would steal even though they knew the penalty if caught would be imprisonment or even losing their hand. The potential fear of loss is overridden by the base need to survive.

When we deprive people of their needs, we cannot expect them to be operating at their full capacity, and this deprivation causes genuine mental stress that can have lasting effects. When we are in this state, we are literally doing whatever we can to make it through the day. And the danger that exists within the charity model in most of our communities is that it caters to survival and not success. For example, we place food resources throughout the community: Someone might get breakfast at a church on the west side of town but then they must travel miles back to the downtown area to get lunch and then they are forced to choose between going to their social security meeting or making it over to the east side to get dinner. When a person is struggling for survival, they will often put off what is best for the long-term (i.e. going to their social security meeting) and instead chase after yet another meal. So here we find what is known as the repetitive economy of survival. Wake up each day and make the never-ending trek of scavenging for food, a blanket, and a place to lay your head for the night that is hopefully safe.

If our call, our vocation in life, is to help our fellow humans and bring to them the good news, then how can we do that if all we are giving them is the moderately alright news, often peppered with more bad news? As a society we have become alright with providing the basic needs and that is all. What we see in the great race that those experiencing homeless endure is that they are more than willing to do what it takes to make their lives better. They are willing to wake up each day at dawn and play according to the rules we have set: go here for dinner, here for a shower, and arrive at this place to get your blanket. However, we are never, ever going to feed or blanket someone out of homelessness. What would happen then if, instead of just supplying the basic needs, we took things a step further? What if we actually provided those we care about with the legitimate tools for success? Is it possible to trust other human beings enough to believe, to hope, to endure with them that they will be successful if we just allow them to be themselves while doing it?

This is the underlying problem that has become the most damning part of our non-profit sector; we stopped thinking that people will be successful if just given the chance, a second chance to do it right. Now, that doesn't mean people will be perfect or that they will never stumble. But our love should be there unconditionally, ready to catch folks when they are falling and always ready to pick them back up if they do hit the ground again. How we accomplish ending any injustice we are fighting will be found in the very basic principles of living out our charity to its fullest extent. Charity—*agape*—is emulating the love of God towards all people. It is forever forgiving, guiding, and encompassing.

The answer to the question of how to find a cure to any problem we face within the non-profit sector is found in accepting people where they are and supplying them what they need.

Come as You Are

For far too long our system of charity has been based upon a broken model of client sufficiency and not practical solutions. We've required people to reach a certain level of wholeness before they are even considered fit to be served. Sure, we will give out food, but if they want to surpass having their basic needs met, they've got to prove they want it. The truth is humans just don't work that way. We can't go after what we truly need until we've had our needs truly met. So, instead of requiring people to be perfect before receiving, we have to remember what the scriptures tell us: "Freely you have received, freely give," and, "give to the one who asks of you, and do not refuse the one who would borrow from you." These are difficult passages, but they teach us what we are called to do: To accept people right where they are, believing in who they can become and not judging them based upon temporal circumstances.

Unfortunately, so many of our non-profits have prohibitive requirements the exclude massive portions of the population who are in need. We force them to go to chapel services or to submit to drug and alcohol testing in order to receive our services. We impose a certain level of perfection on people that God doesn't require of any of us to receive Divine Love. God doesn't say, "Be perfect and then come to me." Rather, God simply said, "Let them come to me." This is grace and mercy personified.

What benefit is there in turning a person away when they are at the base of their brokenness? This has become an acceptable norm within the culture of charity. I watched in horror one night as people were being turned away into the cold because they were required to take a breathalyzer test before they could enter a cold weather shelter. What benefit is there in that? Are we saying that having a substance abuse problem is worthy of the death penalty? Yet, we see it happen all across our nation as people are turned away for multiple reasons from the places that are tasked with being the last ditch safety net for those who have lost everything.

When we first opened our cold weather shelter for families, people looked at me like I had lost my marbles when I said we would have no intake rules. "We will take people just as they are, as many as we can legally fit in the building." (And sometimes there were a few more than that.) We took folks without question or hesitation. If they were in need of shelter, we would take them in. They only thing that could cause someone to have to leave was if they committed a violent crime and we were forced to engage law enforcement. Otherwise, they were welcome in our doors, in our home.

The immediate thing we saw was how the clients themselves reacted to this unconditional love. Instead of attempting to push the envelope, we built a level of mutual respect. Instead of telling people what to do, we would ask them why they did the things they did. Instead of doing everything for them, we found ways for them to participate in their own success. It was in building relationships where we could have those difficult conversations that real change began to take place. Our guests would tell us what they needed, what they wanted, what was holding them back from achieving success. So with each unique situation that was brought forward to us, we would try to find equally unique ways to respond to their personal needs.

It was substantially more difficult, there's no doubt about it. Turning away people who are hard to handle will, without question, make your life easier, but the result will always be the same: people will remain living on the streets. Instead of allowing that to continue, we can simply reject the notion that some people are unworthy. We can realize that we are all, even on the worst day of our brokenness, made in the image of God. We bear the likeness of our Heavenly Parent. So in this we must fight with that same passion and love for those who have been rejected by society (or intentionally designed to fail within it) and create a pathway forward.

Christ tells us, "Whatever you have done to the least of these, who are my siblings, you are doing it to me." So, when we reject someone from receiving our care, we are rejecting not just them but Christ himself. And when we receive someone who is in need, we are receiving Christ into our midst. This same principle exists within nearly every religion, the idea that by respecting the dignity of other humans, and even all of creation, we are respecting the divinity that exists within all who call this place home.

We are called in our love to endure with those we care about. That does not just mean in their moments of clarity but most especially when things are not going well. Living out First Corinthians 13 in our daily lives, living in the fullness of charity means that we are to walk alongside everyone with that agape love. We are to abide with them in patience and kindness. We are to endure. And that means we have to follow through to the completion of the race. It will not be easy; as a matter of fact, I can assure you it will be very difficult at times. There will be nights when it might even feel unbearable, that the burden is just too much.

I remember one such night when one of our volunteers had called in sick and I had to go up to the shelter in the wee hours of the night, only to find that the couch where the volunteers normally slept after lights out had been given to a mother and her son who had been kicked out of their home by an abusive spouse. I found a mat that wasn't being used and set it up in the kitchen and slept that night with two inches of old foam separating me from the cold, hard floor. I woke up that next morning cold and stiff and angry. The child sleeping on the couch with his mother woke up very early that day, screaming with confusion and fear. For two weeks, they slept on that couch awaiting a room to become available for them within the shelter. The mother would wake up in the middle of the night and sneak out to have a cigarette. Volunteers began to complain about how they couldn't sleep and that they needed their rest to make it to work the next day. Slowly volunteers began to fall by the wayside and so more and more nights I was spending up there at the shelter sleeping on a mat in the kitchen and waking up the next day to do my daily responsibilities managing the facility.

Then, one day, in a moment of clarity, that mother went out and found a job, she slowly saved her money and eventually a room became available for her to move into. Peace was restored at the shelter and a month later she had saved enough to put a deposit on a small apartment near her work. And as of the time of this writing she is still working at that same restaurant and her son is now growing up with a sense of security, all because we endured with her to the bitter end. As a matter of fact, 100% of the families who stayed with us that bitter winter found permanent housing before spring rolled around.

What I had to remember was that the mat I was sleeping on was the same as the ones we were providing to our clients. My discomfort was their discomfort, except I had an exit strategy. When it was all said and done, I still had a home to go to. We work so hard to avoid discomfort, but sometimes it is the most necessary thing to achieving the success that we want for ourselves, for our clients, and for our world. Someone's discomfort caused them to set a log on fire; that is innovation. Entrepreneurship found a way to manufacture that heat and created first fireplaces, stoves, and eventually A/C units for heating and cooling. And charity? If we learn from our partners in industry, we will create a way that everyone can be warm.

Housing First

There are as many different stories about how a person becomes homeless as there are people to tell those stories, but there is one reassuring theme amongst them all, one root cause of their homelessness, and it is not drugs or alcohol. It's that they don't have a house. That is quite simply what causes homelessness, becoming house-less. That means that the cure is equally as simple, putting someone in a house. Now, this is certainly a scandalous suggestion. Why should we be responsible for taking care of another person's housing? Well, at the risk of sounding trite, because the Bible says so. We are called time and again to take care of the needs of those whom we see struggling. But if the good book isn't quite enough of a selling point, housing people is also a hell of a lot cheaper than quite literally everything else we are doing right now. Oh, and it's immensely successful.

When you take the cost of a person living on the streets at any given moment, from utilizing the hospital for basic healthcare needs (or just as another form of shelter) to incarceration for basic survival techniques like sleeping outside, and all of the other services that a person might access in order to make it through the day, it costs a tremendous amount of money. Some estimates say that the average homeless person costs a community more than $60,000 dollars a year, just to live on the streets. Whereas, for a fraction of that cost (1/3 to be exact) we can provide that same person with housing, food, and case management so that they can truly get their lives back on track.

What is remarkable about this simple idea is that is has been so successful in the communities who have adopted the model. When people are placed in housing using a "come as you are" mentality, they are starting to become actualizers of their own success. No longer burdened with the fear of day-to-day survival, they are able to utilize that wasted energy toward productive things like looking for a job, qualifying for social services, and generally getting their lives back on track.

Even in those rare cases where a person might never better themselves, the community is still saving major dollars simply by housing the person versus allowing them to stay on the streets.

I received a call once from a man with a very gruff attitude. "I'm not some bleeding heart liberal, you understand. But I'm looking around and thinking ... there's got to be something better than this for these people." He's absolutely right, on both accounts. You don't have to be a bleeding heart liberal to see the effectiveness of data. As the saying goes, numbers don't lie. Communities that have begun to implement a Housing First model are seeing lives changed and money saved and that appeals to both the most bleeding heart liberal and also the most tightly fisted fiscal conservative.

What has made the model successful has been the innovative idea of having what's known as the "come as you are" method. When we remove the impediments that are preventing people from seeking shelter, more people will. And the more people who come in the higher our success will be. For far too long we've used a screening method, basically with the intention of weeding out difficult clients and hopefully only gathering up those folks who will be easy to rehouse. The problem is this hasn't worked out very well—not for the clients, the community or for the charities utilizing this model. Sure, it looks great on paper to say, "We've got a 90-day program that will bring our clients from (perceived) failure to (standardized) success!" But this type of cookie cutter ideology cuts away the rest of the dough and discards it, even though it's just as good and worthy.

And who hasn't tried a 90-day method in their own life? 90 days to the perfect abs! 30 days to your better you! And what happens? You skip a few days, and then you feel like a failure. So you tell yourself, "I'll pick up again tomorrow," and maybe you do. But most of us don't and then slowly those 90 days slip away and we feel like we've failed. What's so funny is many of my friends who have failed at these types of programs will tell me that they did so because they began to feel the pressure, as each day slipped by they started to feel a bit of anxiety. Maybe they realized that they didn't have the same body type as the models used to sell the original product and they were reaching for a goal that was unobtainable from the very beginning. This same feeling is what floods the minds of our clients, except what's at stake is not whether or not they will have a sexy six pack but the sustainability of a home. That's a hell of a lot scarier of a proposition.

When we create a system that takes folks just as they are and believes in them, they begin to believe in themselves. Sure, it's a lot harder, but it means we become like the personal trainer who wakes you up in the morning and says, "Alright! You can do this. You could only do 30 pushups yesterday, but I know you can do 35 today." Housing First takes it a step further; it goes ahead and gives you the beach body to begin with. It says, "Here's everything you've lost, this is your second chance and we are going to walk alongside you, encouraging you, to show you how to maintain this life."

This same method of loving people into success has been used in every form of the non-profit sector with tremendous success, from Patch Adams' Gesunheit! Institute to Johann Hari's radical expose, Chasing the Scream, which fundamentally transforms the way in which we address drug addiction. When we approach someone in love, genuine, raw, and radical love, we don't say, "You'll live outside until you learn your lesson!" but instead we say, "I'm going to take you inside until we figure out what broke and we are going to find a way to fix it, together."

One of my dear friends, mentors, and sojourners in this work of justice, Shane Claiborne, says, "We give people fish, we teach them how to fish, we tear down the walls that have been built up around the fish pond and we figure out who polluted it." That is the very core principle of love, to take on the whole cause, not just portions of it. Not just the easy parts but the difficult bits as well. How do we do this? For those of us addressing homelessness, it is in supplying them housing. It's that simple but also that difficult.

In your wing of the beautiful world of charity, there is also a simple solution. Someone is right now revolutionizing it and screaming about it from the rooftops and there are people fighting against it, kicking against change. But I'm here to tell you change will come. It always does. It's time to stop fighting against these simple truths and accept them with grace and love. It might not be easiest for us, but it will be easier for our clients, and that's really who we are doing this for. And if you aren't, I say with true love and compassion for you if you cannot endure to the end with those whom you are tasked with serving, then it might be time to find where you are really called to be because this might not be it.

CHAPTER TWELVE

Charity Never Ends

Love is not patronizing and charity isn't about pity, it is about love. Charity and love are the same — with charity you give love, so don't just give money but reach out your hand instead.
Mother Teresa

A Beginning to an End

One of my mentors once said to me, "There will never be an end to the injustices that man can think up, our work is never done." They were certainly correct, but the injustices do change with time. Over time, every issue is given its day in the societal court in order to fight for justice and liberation. Our culture looks at these issues and says, "We will no longer tolerate this injustice," but it seems as soon as we close the door on one, we quickly find the next door open that we must run though in order to bring that same peace and comfort that those of us with privilege are already enjoying. With each brick that is laid in the road to justice, we must not forget the labor or the laborers who placed those bricks there. We must continue to carry their torch, working all day and through the night. An equally important part of this task is to know the time when we are supposed to pass the torch.

On the evening before his death, Dr. King gave one of his most impassioned speeches known as "The Mountain Top Speech". He was speaking to union workers in Tennessee and, though his message was originally a rousing call to arms, it quickly took a biblical turn. "I would like to live a long life: longevity has its place. But I'm not concerned with that now. I just want to do God's will. And He's allowed me to go up to the mountain. And I've looked over. And I've seen the Promised Land. I may not go there with you. But I want you to know, tonight, that we, as a people, will get to the Promised Land. So I'm happy, tonight. I'm not worried about anything. I'm not fearing any man. Mine eyes have seen the glory of the coming of the Lord!" In those prophetic (and possibly foreknowing) words, Dr. King passed the torch. He was assassinated the next day.

He harkened back to that biblical narrative of another leader, Moses, who brought his people so far but could not go all the way. His purpose, like Dr. King's, was to bring others to the foot of the Promised Land. But it would be Aaron, and others, who would conquer the land, who would see the vision through. Then there would be others, countless others, who would come after them to continue in that mantle.

It is alright to let go, to pass the torch, to sit on the mountain top and watch others walk in. We do not, individually, have to see every single victory. It's impossible. What we can do is hold the torch, lay the bricks, and light the way along the path we build so that others may build further upon it. This great change brings about new forms of liberation for those whom we have all been called to serve, no matter in which demographic of charity we are called to do it. But the one thing we cannot do is become lost in the desert of ideology and self-importance. A day will come when even the words I'm writing now will be obsolete and others will create new ways of trudging forward into the new battles that will need to be fought. And to that end, I bless their future endeavor, even if it undoes those things that I, or any of us, have done before.

The problem with our non-profit industrial complex is that we've become too afraid of actually fixing the problem, as if somehow our purpose will go away and, even worse, for those of us who work in the field, our revenue source will go away. The incentive for success has almost been destroyed entirely because succeeding at our job means, in essence, to end our job. It's like asking a baker to make a loaf of bread that will ensure no one is ever hungry again. It would certainly be a noble thing to do, end world hunger, but it would also mean that people would eventually never need to buy bread from you, or anyone, ever again. You would be liberating others and damning yourself in the process. This is the very reason why our charity model no longer works. We are just as much in need of the clients as they are of us. And so the cycle continues.

Because we've allowed charity to be defined as a finite thing, an institution as opposed to an action, we have painted ourselves into a corner of no longer having the ability to look at the problem with a desire to create an actual solution. We forget that we should always look for the solution because once we finally fix the problem before us, a new one will always present itself. Just as the baker invents the bread that will end hunger, surely he will look around and realize that now that everyone can eat it is time to find out how they will also drink.

Breaking the Cycle

We have to stop looking at charity as something that will go away once the task at hand is completed and rather as a fluid conversation within our culture about what injustices we must confront next. We break this cycle by no longer allowing ourselves to be bound to one thing and instead looking at the intersectionality of what we hope to overcome as a people. Once we find a cure for cancer, we will need to find a way to make sure that everyone has equal and fair access to treatment. Once that access is granted, someone will have to be the group that holds future generations responsible for holding true to that ideal. The work never ends, it simply evolves. So we must stop fearing the end of our work and instead find ways to make our work fluid. That is where we end our own dependency on the structure.

If we truly create a model that ends homelessness and propels us toward a society that honors fair housing, then we should not fear losing our job by actually solving the problem. Instead, we should be thankful that we've created a world that guarantees everyone a place to live, because that will include us. A society that values the work of all people, which includes our clients, will also value our place in this new order as well. We will be creating the world in which we can all live with equality and peace. I do not say this in a utopian sense, there will always be struggle. On the contrary, I say this in the least utopian way possible.

I once took my car in to have antifreeze put in as a hard freeze was coming. I had the system flushed and new fluids put in. As I drove home, a hose busted and it cracked my radiator. By attempting to fix the problem, I had created a new one. As it turns out, the fix also found all the other cracks and holes in the system. The same is true for genuine charity that seeks after justice. When we patch one thing, it will apply pressure into areas we didn't even know we should be looking at. This is the beauty of the innovation of humankind, we harness electricity but then we are forced to ask the fundamental questions of supply and demand and the philosophical questions of access. May we strive in life to be a Nikola Telsa over a Thomas Edison.

When I first began my journey of working for the homeless, I never would have known how many different issues all had a touching point with homelessness. The intersections of justice did not seem, to my untrained eye, to collide, but they certainly did. Domestic violence, discrimination against the LGBTQ+ community, failures within the public school system, environmental concerns, workers' rights, and the list goes on in a never-ending cycle of injustice that brings the poor, the working class, and even the millionaire to their knees. All of these unique issues that seem to stand on their own all meet at the intersection of homelessness and poverty.

Domestic violence is not something unique to homelessness; it is something experienced in homes all across the world, rich or poor. This social justice issue affects individuals and families regardless of social status, race or religion. However, it can be a doorway into homelessness, just as so many other issues can be. If we are able to address the root cause of homelessness—not having access to a home—then those individuals who experience domestic violence that leads them to homelessness no longer have to fear because we've created a system where there is a safety net that catches them and instantly re-houses them. Imagine a world where victims of domestic violence are able to walk out the door, no longer allowing the fear of finances or housing to hold them back. It removes a certain power from the abuser and puts it into the hands of the abused. They can no longer lord over them the fear of living on the streets.

Does this fix every aspect of the control structure that exists in every situation of domestic violence? No, but at the intersection of domestic violence and homelessness, it certainly does. It closes that road and one portion of the problem is now solved. The task, for charity, becomes then to move on to the other intersections, knowing we've solved a portion of the problem and we can then focus the rest of our energy on the next task.

So even if we are to take on the cause of truly ending homelessness in our communities, this just opens wide the chasm of what we shall end next. What will be the evolution of our purpose as we grow and elevate from one purpose and on to the next? Once we cure our culture of allowing homelessness to exist, we can, without fear or hesitation, move on to the next injustice we have been exposed to in the process that exists upon the large wheel of disparity. Ending homelessness, or any society ill, should not be something we fear but something we run after with reckless abandon.

A Never-Ending Story

There is no reason to fear the inevitable reality of change because living out charity as a daily lifestyle means that we are able to live in the fullness of the love we are called to have for all humankind. Sure, the issues will change and that is alright. Human beings are remarkably adaptable creatures when given the opportunity. What we must work toward together is to stop fighting against change and instead fight boldly for it. No matter where you are on this journey, client, volunteer, donor or staff, you can help bring needed change to your community. We all have a responsibility to strive to be better. I'll be the first to admit it won't be easy. Nothing worthwhile ever is.

But we accepted this responsibility knowing it wouldn't be easy. Sure, most of us didn't know how hard it would be when we first took up this calling. I know I didn't. When I first walked into a small park in the center of town with my father, holding a box of chicken, I had no idea what I was getting myself into. I could have never imagined that in a few short weeks we would be surrounded by police cars being summoned to City Hall.

I could not have seen then, as we stood in line at a local supermarket making our order, that this would begin a lifelong passion. I could never have known that the visit to City Hall would become one of hundreds, where this battle would eventually take me from serving food on the streets to operating a shelter a decade later. Nor did I know that as I was cutting my teeth on these unskilled speeches before my local government it would one day prepare me to sit with senators and governors, to address them on the broader issues of homelessness. I couldn't see it, and maybe if I could have, I would have run away all those years ago. I'm glad I couldn't see it all, but I am eternally grateful that it brought me here.

Long before they called me "Chicken-Man" on the streets of Pensacola, this journey began with a scared young boy standing next to his mother as she cried. She was powerless and so was I, even more so. She cried because injustice had met our family that day as we were escorted out of the motel room that my father could not afford. What no one within this system could see was that my father was on the other side of town, finally employed and at his first day of work, a detail I would not know for many years. There was so much I could not see from my limited stature as a young homeless boy, but I could see the pain. In my heart that day I promised myself that I would do something. I could not have ever imagined it would be this. As many pathways as I have walked down in my life, of all of them I am forever and eternally thankful I took the one that brought me here, just as I am sure that each of you are thankful as well that you took your journey that brought you into this wonderful work of charity.

We have all asked many questions: *Why do I do this? Am I doing this the best way? Have I really changed anything?*

This answer is undoubtedly yes. It is easy for us to be clouded by the alleged failures we see every single day. For every client that is a success story we know that there are countless others that are not. My hope in writing this, and in you taking the time to read it, is that we will take that age-old parable to heart; it is time to leave the ninety-nine to seek after the lost sheep. We must fight, like never before, to find ways to embolden our causes to no longer pander to what is easy but chase after the difficult cases. We must innovate, revolutionize, and propel our industry into the next level. Allow your ingenuity to build upon itself into an entrepreneur spirit that will stay up that extra hour, bleed a little more, and never, ever give up—because love never fails.

So what then can we take away from the exegesis of First Corinthians 13? Is it possible that we have truly looked at one of the most popular verses in the Bible completely wrong? I would say the answer is undoubtedly yes, we have. But instead of feeling shame for this or fighting against it simply because it doesn't fit within what we were raised to think, we need to just embrace our new reality and move forward in that understanding that these verses, written by Paul nearly two thousand years ago, are a call to action, not just a sweet thing to say as we embark on married life. It's bigger and bolder than that. They are words written to the whole body, the universal bride. A call to love for all people.

We should also not fear what this means for what our charities can and will become. We should not fear our favorite charity closing because it completed its goal! That should be our pure objective, to close the doors of our charities because we cured cancer, provided fresh drinking water to our communities or because we ended homelessness in our nation. This should be the 100% focus of each and every charity, to bring that chapter to a close and begin a new one, always looking towards the future, always being the conduit for change. We will never lose the ability to find something new to strive after, another purpose within this great focus to bring hope. So let's no longer allow the fear of losing something we are familiar with hold us back from actually completing the goal of curing the ailments we see in the world and instead embrace the knowledge that, "for everything there is a season, and a time for every purpose under heaven," because in the last:

Charity never ends because charity is love.

About Nathan Monk

Nathan Monk is social justice advocate, author, and former Orthodox priest. He lives in Pensacola, FL with his three children. He is the author of *Chasing the Mouse*, a memoir about childhood homelessness, and works with nonprofits and local governments to address issues associated with homelessness, poverty, and social justice.

Having experienced homelessness with his family during his teenage years, Nathan has gone on to found numerous programs providing food, clothing, emergency resources, and shelter. Over the years he has worked with business professionals and government officials to help bring success to their philanthropic work.

Currently, Nathan is the executive director of a nonprofit focused on housing solutions. He is also the founder of the Charity Institute, a consulting firm assisting non-profits. He serves as a board member of the Homelessness and Housing Alliance and the Planning Board of the City of Pensacola. Over his career, he has received notable awards, appointments, and national media for his accomplishments in the area of social justice.

Nathan is also an active public speaker and author. Through writing and speaking, he seeks to educate the public and break down stereotypes in our culture about people experiencing poverty and homelessness. His expanded educational programs and consulting work help create nonprofit cultures that are truly client-oriented. With a focus on outcomes over outreach, Nathan believes we can end homelessness.

Nathan Monk is active on social media…

Follow
@FatherNathan

to get updates

facebook.com/FatherNathan
twitter.com/FatherNathan
instagram.com/FatherNathan
www.CharityInstitute.com

Made in the USA
Middletown, DE
18 November 2019